Silvio

Congressman for Everyone
A Biographical Portrait of Silvio O. Conte
By Peter E. Lynch

SUNSTONE
PRESS

SANTA FE
New Mexico

Sunstone books may be purchased for educational, business, or sales promotional use. For information please write: Special Markets Department, Sunstone Press, P.O. Box 2321, Santa Fe, New Mexico 87504-2321.

FIRST EDITION

10 9 8 7 6 5 4 3 2 1

Library of Congress Cataloging in Publication Data:

Lynch, Peter E., 1945—
    Silvio: congressman for everyone / Peter E. Lynch. — 1st ed.
      p. cm.
    Includes index.
    ISBN: 0-86534-256-3
    1. Conte, Silvio O. (Silvio Ottavio), 1921-1991. 2. legistltors—United States—Biography. 3. United States. Congress. House—Biography. I. Title.
E840. 8. C667L96   1997
328. 73' 092—dc 20   96-44316
[B]   CIP

Published by   SUNSTONE PRESS
                        Post Office Box 2321
                        Santa Fe, NM 87504-2321 / USA
                        (505) 988-4418 / *orders only* (800) 243-5644
                        FAX (505) 988-1025

To Corinne L. Conte, Silvio's beloved wife
who took care of Silvio and their family and was his friend, helper,
campaigner, advisor, strategist, case worker and anchor.

CONTENTS

"He was a Fourth of July parade with all the bells and whistles. With his bright smile and booming laugh, he roared down the highway of life . . . personality as colorful as the fall foliage in his Berkshires."

—Senator Edward M. Kennedy, 1991

"It is the belief in higher presence, a greater good, that enables us to achieve notable things in life."

—Silvio O. Conte, 1989

PREFACE

*I*nitially, this book was to be a collection of humorous anecdotes about Massachusetts Congressman Silvio O. Conte. Interviews and research produced hundreds of amusing tales and, at the same time, painted a picture of an extraordinary Congressional career of hard work, dedication, joy and service to constituents, Massachusetts and the nation. In an era marked by citizens' alienation from their government, Congressman Conte gave his constituents extremely personal representation. As he said in 1989, "I never wanted to come home and have someone say my Office had not been any help." In the process of providing help, Silvio Conte learned the problems and views of his people and used this to shape legislation and national policy.

The purpose of this book is to benefit the Education Foundation which Silvio Conte established a few months prior to his death in early 1991. The author, working for the Housatonic Railroad, came to know Congressman Conte because of his support for a track rehabilitation project for the Housatonic located in his district in Western Massachusetts.

Because many people were so generous with their time and willing to share their recollections of Silvio Conte, this book was a great joy to research and write. For this I am deeply grateful. First I thank the Conte family for their time, help and friendship-Silvio's wife, Corinne; his daughters, Michelle Webb, Sylvia Certo and Gayle Fowler; his son John Conte; his sisters Elisabeth Baldessarini, Sylvia Reid and Angela Bowerman. Next I thank his friends and neighbors whom he served for so many years—most particularly his boyhood friend Dr. Robert Cella who gave continued support, assistance and encouragement along with a number of good dinners. I thank Silvio's many colleagues in Washington—most particularly his closest friend, the late Speaker Thomas P. "Tip" O'Neill, who in two interviews told some of the most entertaining as well as informative Conte stories.

This book would not have been possible without the help of many Congressional staff people whom I especially thank: Nan Donnelly, Sallie Davis, Chinch Wollerton, Jeff Jacobs, Missi Tessier and Richard Baker who offered help, good advice and much needed encouragement. At home I thank my wife Kathryn and my daughter Kelley for their support and patience. I thank my great pal Jeffrey Price for giving me the idea to write this and I thank Sue Fairbanks and Marilyn Rubitski for their help in getting my scribbling into the computer.

—Peter E. Lynch

THE MAN FROM PITTSFIELD

"The thing I remember about my brother
is that he never forgot that he came
from Pittsfield."

—*Sylvia Reid, Sister*

*T*he first hint of red and orange in the leaves of Western Massachusetts signalled the start of another campaign. Every two years from 1950
to 1990, Corinne, Silvio O. Conte's wife, along with six or eight of her faithful friends would head out at dawn for Adams or Lee or Greenfield. Armed
with Conte leaflets and maybe some campaign trinkets, they went from door
to door with their notebooks. All day long they would say, "Here's a little
paper about Silvio. If you have anything you want him to know, let me take
it down."

The only change through the years was that at first it was hard to
get into living rooms. Later it was hard to get out. The campaign became a
reunion of old friends. After ten or twelve hours Corinne would say, "That's
enough for today. Let's go eat." Then she treated her friends to a good meal
before heading home to Pittsfield, sometimes picking up Silvio who had
just spent hours on the campaign trail himself. He would always say,
"Corinne, Corinne how much did you spend this time? These meals are my
biggest campaign expense. We can't keep spending like this. We need some
new lawn signs because some are starting to look bad because they've been
out for five or six campaigns. All I got was a cheeseburger at Friendly's."

"Well, Sil, that's your fault. We were out all day and deserve a good
meal; besides we're going to have a good time if we're going to work this
hard."

And so went the campaigns of Silvio O. Conte, who was sent four
times to the Massachusetts Senate and seventeen times to the Congress, usually with seventy plus percent of the vote. In a time of pollsters, political

consultants and TV ads when politicians got into homes only on TV, the Contes did it live. Silvio's instructions were always the same: "Corinne, get'em out and just see everybody."

The story begins near Vicenza in Northern Italy at the close of the 19th Century. Hard times were sending many Italians to America. Silvio Lora, leaving his family behind, headed for North Adams, Massachusetts to seek a new life. The tall red haired man was in North Adams for several years before he could send for his family in 1905. As the Lora family journeyed through France to board the ship for New York, Silvio's brother-in-law became ill and was detained along with Silvio's wife, while his two children, ten-year-old Lucia and her seven-year-old brother Tony, were sent on to New York. At Ellis Island Silvio Lora met his children who did not recognize him after so many years of separation. Lucia refused to go with her father and remained at Ellis Island with Tony while their father went back to North Adams to seek the help of a local judge who quickly arranged for their release. Soon Lucia's mother and uncle arrived in North Adams. Not long afterward, Silvio Lora died, making it necessary for his wife to turn their home into a boardinghouse lodging a dozen working men. Through her teenage years, Lucia helped her mother in the boardinghouse with cooking and other chores and also worked in a thread mill a few miles walk away.

In search of work at the age of 17, Ottavio Conte went from Vicenza, Italy to Alsace-Lorraine to work on the German Railway in 1905. There his foot was crushed by a maintenance car and he was hospitalized for six months, during which time he learned German. When discharged from the hospital, he joined the merchant marine which took him to the Panama Canal where he left his ship, worked for a short time and then came to Pennsylvania to work in a coal mine. In 1910 he went north to work on the Hoosac rail tunnel expansion in North Adams, Massachusetts. There he found lodging in the Lora boardinghouse where he met young Lucia. Soon he learned that the Stanley Company, a forerunner of General Electric, was hiring people in Pittsfield, 18 miles to the south. When he went to apply he found that they would not hire Italians. Being fluent in German he hired on as Otto Hoffman. He continued to work for "the GE," as it was called in Pittsfield, for 45 years. He became a foreman in the porcelain shop and was able to bring his parents and three brothers from Italy to Pittsfield. Soon secure in his job, he changed his name back to Ottavio Conte, reclaiming his proud Italian heritage. Once established in Pittsfield, Ottavio Conte married Lucia Lora in 1915 when he was 27 and she was 20. He was a quiet, hard-working, dignified man who, despite only a grade school education, was fluent in Italian, German and English, had a great interest in poetry, history and opera. Lucia and Ottavio's household grew to include three daughters, Elisabeth, Silvia and Angela and one son, the third child, Silvio Ottavio Conte, born in 1921.

The Conte home was typical for a Northern Italian family—it was strongly matriarchal. Because Ottavio worked at "the GE" and then did odd jobs on a farm after hours, Lucia ran the household. The family was a major force in shaping Silvio's personality and character. From his parents he learned hard work. At the age of six Silvio would walk with his mother carrying a burlap bag to a local gas plant to pick up pieces of coke which were the waste products of this process. This fuel would be used to heat their home and cook their meals. Silvio, as a child, helped care for the chickens and rabbits which the family raised for food. When he received his driver's license he would sell chickens and eggs between Pittsfield and North Adams to supplement the family's income. As a teenager Silvio had a summer job on a farm where he did haying and tended to the animals. After a walk of a mile to work, a long day and another mile walk home, Silvio would come home and collapse on the floor, prompting his mother to urge him to quit, but he kept working because he knew the family needed the dollar a day he brought home. During the school year Silvio worked in a neighborhood grocery store stocking shelves after school. Despite the family's dedication to work, the children were carefully supervised and taught a strong sense of responsibility and right and wrong. After a hard day of work the Conte family and friends gathered in Lucia's kitchen to enjoy one of her magnificent meals of homemade pasta, risotto, polenta or a roast. For her entire married life she cooked on a gas fired enamel stove which she would never give up. Lucia's meals were enhanced by Ottavio's homemade wines and the rabbits which he raised feeding them bread cubes and vegetables. During the Great Depression the Contes knew hard times but they also would lend a helping hand to those less fortunate. Lucia, because she had come to America as a young child, was fluent in both English and Italian. Frequently she would assist Italian speaking friends and neighbors with citizenship papers, job applications and other matters for which they required help. Often this assistance was accompanied by a meal and good companionship at Lucia's kitchen table. "Allegria", Italian for good cheer, was often used to describe the Conte home where people were always welcome. From his mother Silvio learned to laugh at a good story or event. One of her favorites was watching Silvio practice to be a prize fighter at age 12 when he stuffed a burlap bag and hung it in the basement for a punching bag, sending his mother and sisters into gales of laughter at his theatric gestures.

Ottavio started to save to send Silvio to college, but the Depression caused occasional layoffs and the family had to spend these savings to survive. In 1937, Ottavio told Silvio that he would not be able to send him on to college and instructed him to take the vocational course at Pittsfield High School. "Become a machinist and work at the GE and you will have a good life." Silvio did not want this, but being dutiful, he acquiesced. Vocational students were separated from the college bound, but Silvio managed to maintain contact with all his fellow students. He joined the track team and set records doing the high hurdles and worked odd jobs on the side. Graduation came in 1940 when Silvio began seven months work at the GE as an apprentice machinist, a job he thoroughly hated. He found another position as an apprentice pressman at the Pittsfield newspaper, *The Berkshire Eagle*, where he worked a few months before entering the Navy.

World War II changed life for Silvio Conte as it did for many other Americans. He enlisted in the Navy Seabees in 1942 and was sent to the South Pacific where he saw duty on Samoa and New Caledonia. In 1944 he contracted a tropical disease, filariasis. He was sent to the hospital in Oakland, California, and to complete his recovery, on to Sun Valley, the Idaho ski resort which had been lent to the government as a military hospital. There he made many new friends and was almost persuaded to settle in Idaho to reap the post-war boom the west was expecting, but Lucia prevailed, telling her son that she would never see him if he lived in Idaho. Silvio returned to Pittsfield in late 1944.

A portion of the new GI Bill of Rights provided 48 months of full college tuition to those with medical problems or disabilities. Silvio applied to Boston College and was accepted to begin the four year course in mid-1945. Acceptance depended upon taking a four month preparatory course in English and mathematics and achieving satisfactory grades, which Silvio did. Because of the large demand for education at the end of the War, the colleges and universities were holding classes throughout the year. This enabled Silvio to complete his Bachelor of Arts requirements in two years and then to enter Boston College Law School right away. The most profound effect this college had on Silvio was that it developed his ability to work extremely hard. In his own words: "The story goes something like this. Forty-five years ago a young Italian American from Pittsfield, born poor in resources but rich in dreams, comes to this campus to make a new life. When he went to law school, he lived in a ratty, roach infested boarding house for five dollars a week. He hitchhiked back and forth to Pittsfield each weekend to be with his family. To make ends meet, that young man worked as a bartender, sold Christmas cards and class rings, and painted houses."

Midway through his college career, Silvio found inspiration when he married Corinne Duval in 1947. Corinne, also from Pittsfield, had served in the Navy during the war as a nurse. She met Silvio in the hospital in Pittsfield where he was having his appendix removed. She was introduced to him by another nurse and began caring for him in the hospital and then continued to care for him for another 44 years. While Silvio was in law school a daughter, Michelle, was born. Corinne could not attend Silvio's law school graduation in 1949 because she was in the hospital in Pittsfield giving birth to their second daughter, Sylvia. Silvio's parents proudly attended the graduation, one of the few times in 50 years that Lucia was persuaded to leave Pittsfield.

Silvio's responsibilities were monumental. He worked as a maintenance man at Philomethia House, a home for retired priests, in return for room and board. He had a 1931 Model A Ford which he used to go back and forth to Pittsfield on weekends and school holidays. When he was home he had little time to be with his family because he worked many different jobs,—house painting, bartending, running a chicken and egg business. The burden almost overwhelmed him. "During my first year in law school I injured myself playing football here at Boston College. The class work, the studying, the jobs, those classes at 18 Tremont Street with no air-conditioning, police sirens screaming, James Michael Curley yelling at the top of his lungs from the street outside never seemed to end. They seemed to go on forever and ever. Well, I ended up with a D in Father O'Reilley's Future Interest course. Father Kenealy took me aside. 'Silvio', he said, 'I think you ought to consider another law school'. I told him that if I couldn't graduate from Boston College, I didn't want to go to any other law school. The work load, the pressure and the responsibility all came to a head that afternoon. But I knew that if he'd give me another chance I could achieve anything. I told him that day that if they would let me stay I would make them proud of me and proud of him one day. He must have believed me because he gave me that second chance. I ended up graduating in the top third of that class."

Out of Boston College, Silvio had to earn a living to support his family. The year of his graduation, 1949, was not an opportune time to seek work because the country was in a recession. Silvio began to practice law, working in John Alberti's office in North Adams. The weekly salary of twenty-five dollars was not enough to support his family and he needed more income. When the 1950 census began, he sought the lead census job in Berkshire County. Silvio went to the Democratic State Senator, Mike Condron, and received a tacit understanding that the job would be his. When the job was awarded to another, Silvio decided to challenge this three-term, popular incumbent in the Democratic primary. Thwarted in this, Silvio joined the Republican Party to run against Condron. For many years afterward he felt that the Democrats always favored the Irish over the Italians.

Silvio, his family and friends were all new to politics with the exception of his father-in-law, Charlie Duval, a staunch Republican. Family and friends gathered in a Pittsfield office to plot strategy. Silvio's parents were apprehensive about his candidacy, fearing disgrace if he lost, but Corinne encouraged him and told his parents that he had great talent and much to offer. Ottavio soon became avidly interested in the campaign and checked the papers every day, becoming upset if anyone said anything negative. He urged his daughters and friends to attend all of Silvio's functions. Silvio's charm and ability for hard work came into full bloom in this race. His energy allowed him to campaign from dawn until late at night. His personality made it easy for him to approach strangers and ask for their vote. The devotion of his family and friends led them to work long hours and enjoy the campaigns. Not only were his family and friends tireless and dedicated, but they were also well organized. They were able to divide up the territory ward by ward or town by town; their energies were always channelled efficiently. They distributed a blotter showing a family picture and the slogan "a statesman not a politician" as they combed the district. So diligent were his volunteers that they felt guilty if one house was missed, and years later told stories of walking up hilly driveways a quarter mile long to ask for a vote and being told "I'd have to vote for someone whose supporter would walk way up here." Fund raisers in 1950 were coffee hours where for fifty cents or a dollar one got a cup of coffee and a little card from the Silvio O. Conte Club.

On election night his family and supporters gathered in Lucia's kitchen to hear the results on the radio. As the ward results came in, victory was assured at 10 p.m. Neighbors brought over more food as more and more people arrived. Some brought gifts of watches, radios, etc., as tribute for the Senator-elect, all of which he promptly returned. When the final vote tallies were complete, Silvio had won 55.4% of the vote against the Democratic incumbent, significant because it was one Republican bright spot in an otherwise strong Democratic year and also because his victory broke a 20 - 20 tie in the Massachusetts Senate.

The State Senate was supposed to be part time work, but not for Silvio. His district was the farthest from Boston and he could not go home each night as most colleagues did. He had to stay in Boston from Monday morning until Thursday evening when the Senate recessed. On Friday, Saturday and Sunday he worked in his law office in Pittsfield, doing both client and constituent work. One aspect of constituent work to which Silvio devoted great energy was assisting college students get summer jobs.

Close friend and later law partner, Jack Martin, recalls that the first time he met Silvio was on a trip to his Pittsfield office in search of summertime work. Expecting a formal, conservatively dressed older man as Senator, Jack found Silvio dressed in a flannel shirt and old pants wearing red suspenders and smoking a corncob pipe. When he walked into the office Silvio said, "whaddya want, kid?" Jack soon had a summer job at the Highway Department. Silvio subsequently found him jobs throughout his college and law school days. As a freshman Senator he became chairman of two committees, Insurance and Constitutional Law. He also got to know his life long friend, Tip O'Neill, who was Speaker of the Massachusetts House. Despite being from opposing parties they worked together to get legislation passed. Silvio, unusual for a Republican, worked for legislation to increase the minimum wage to seventy-five cents an hour and to clean up the state's rivers by reducing pollution.

This new life was hectic. He still did not have as much time as he would have liked for his family. His mother, who viewed going to Boston the same as crossing the ocean, complained that Silvio did not come to see her often enough. "But Ma, I have many appointments to keep and many people to help." "Never mind that, I'm still your mother and you should come see me often." He requested a timely end to the 1951 session because "I have been away so long I have to introduce myself to my wife and children." His third child, John, was born a year after Silvio graduated from Boston College and his fourth child, Gayle, arrived three years later.

His law career took a back seat to his senatorial work but he did do some legal work, including representing a young man accused of receiving stolen property. At this first court trial, Silvio's friend, Bob Cella, who attended the trial, said Silvio argued so eloquently that even though he lost the case the young man received a very short sentence. Silvio said, "I guess I did pretty good because his father paid me right away and we became friends." Despite Silvio's education and position as a rising State Senator, he was looked down upon by some fellow Republicans because his speech was not as polished as theirs. He said "-in'" for "—ing" and he had trouble pronouncing certain words. But his friend Bob Cella defended Silvio saying, "He didn't go to Hotchkiss and Yale the way you did. He was raising chickens, he did it all himself."

Democratic Governor Dever made efforts to find a strong opponent to run against Silvio, whom he viewed as a problem. Yet when the 1952 election season began, Silvio had a good record to present to the voters. He had a voting record of 100% and had attended every committee meeting. He had become well known in his district and received the Republican nomination without opposition. He was challenged by Democratic State Representative James McAndrews, who made some attacks but was not able to mount much of a challenge. Silvio used one of his best political skills in this race—the ability to turn political attacks to his advantage. At the East Side Club in Adams, Silvio was repeatedly booed while speaking and looked out at the audience and saw that the heckler was Mike McAndrews, his opponent's brother. Silvio looked right at him and said, "If you want to debate me, Mike, come up on the platform, otherwise keep quiet." Then Silvio pointed out that he had authored more legislation in two years than his opponent had in six. The election results were not even close: Silvio got 72.5% of the votes.

Silvio occupied an unique position in the Massachusetts Senate because his election gave the Republicans a one vote majority during all four terms he served. He continued to advocate progressive legislation and authored a bill providing accident and health insurance to state, city and town employees throughout Massachusetts. He honed his political skills by serving and meeting with his constituents frequently. Corinne began addressing Christmas cards in July. In 1954 he received almost 74% of the vote and in 1956 received the nomination of both the Republicans and the Democrats.

When Congressman James Heselton announced that he would not seek an eighth term in November 1958, Silvio, now the best known Republican in Western Massachusetts, announced his candidacy for the First District seat. His Democratic opponent was the renowned Williams College professor, James MacGregor Burns, who had just completed the widely acclaimed biography of the late President Franklin Delano Roosevelt. This book, *The Lion and The Fox*, gave Burns nationwide stature. He had also assisted John F. Kennedy with his book, *Profiles in Courage*. Senator Kennedy, now being mentioned as a possible Presidential contender in 1960, gave his endorsement to Professor Burns. Burns attracted numerous celebrities to campaign events—film stars Anne Bancroft and Dana Andrews attended a fund raiser in his behalf. In contrast, Silvio had seven Boston Red Sox players at a Holyoke rally.

Silvio followed his Senate strategy, replicating his Berkshire County organization in Franklin, Hampshire and Hampden Counties along with a little of Worcester County. He personally would get out and see as many people as he could in 14 hour days. He and his followers built an organization by meeting and recruiting people from city wards and local neighborhoods in the smaller towns. He began in Holyoke, the largest city in the district. A meeting room was engaged at the Roger Smith Hotel to hold an evening rally. When a dozen people showed up a reporter asked, "How are you going to get elected if only 12 people come?" Silvio replied, "You just come back next week." For the rest of the evening Silvio and his people went to police stations, fire houses, the French Club, the Irish Club, the Polish Club, etc., and asked people to come to a rally next week and bring a friend or relative. People were asked where they lived and soon Silvio had found supporters on every block of each ward. Enroute home to Pittsfield at 3 a.m., Silvio sat back and puffed on his cigar and said to his longtime pal, "Jesus, Jake, we chopped a lotta wood tonight." A week later the next rally was held and hundreds of people showed up, so many that they could not all fit into the large meeting room. This made Holyoke one of his favorite cities —the only one that ever got him to change his name. For 364 days each year he was Silvio O. Conte, the Italian from Pittsfield, but on St. Patrick's Day he became Silvio O'Conte, the Irishman from Holyoke, where he marched every March 17th for thirty years at the head of the parade with big green O'Conte signs. It was rumored that he got some votes in Holyoke because some people actually thought he was Irish.

In the midst of the 1958 campaign an international crisis erupted, bringing the threat of American involvement in Pacific warfare. China threatened two small islands, Quemoy and Matsu, in the Strait of Formosa, and it was thought that an attack on Taiwan might bring American involvement. Professor Burns and his supporters said that this crisis underscored Burns's superior qualifications plus an extensive knowledge of foreign affairs necessary to serve in Congress. Burns intimated that Silvio did not know where Quemoy and Matsu were and had no ideas for handling this crisis. Silvio was accused of waffling because he made no definitive statements. He did not know what to do about these two islands and was in good company, because President Eisenhower, the Department of State and the Joint Chiefs of Staff did not know what to do either. Finally, after having been bombarded with much criticism, he spoke out at a dinner in late September and said, "I intend to wage a clean and hard campaign. I will present my own ideas on foreign and domestic legislative matters that come up in Congress. I will not seek to give anyone in the First Congressional District the impression that as a neophyte Congressman I can set foreign policy." This infuriated Burns's people but made sense to the electorate.

The campaign was not without acrimony. Professor Burns proposed that there be seven debates between the candidates. He was on leave from his professorship but Silvio was still a Senator and replied, "Needless to say I cannot accept your cordial invitation to engage in a debate because I have been shuttling back and forth from Boston to my home and then out into the 84 cities and towns." Burns was irate because Silvio refused to debate, preferring as always to get out and see the people. Silvio was not pleased because Burns's invitation got to the press before he received it. There were charges that Silvio was less than supportive of labor because he had not backed all state legislation desired by the AFL-CIO, but he received the support of the Brotherhood of Railroad Trainmen which had a large membership in the district.

Two days before the election snow fell in the Berkshires, but the sun shone brightly on Election Day which proved to be a disaster for the Republicans—both in Massachusetts, where they lost nearly every office, and across the country where 47 House seats and 13 Senate seats were lost. But the First Massachusetts Congressional District remained Republican. The Conte strategy of getting out and seeing the voters worked. He received 55.4% of the vote, branded by the papers as a landslide, and won a majority of the vote in all but seven of the 84 towns and cities in the District, even carrying Burns's hometown of Williamstown. Silvio may have been unsure of the location of Quemoy and Matsu, but he knew where Holyoke and Greenfield were.

MASSACHUSETTS CONGRESSMAN

"To Silvio the constituents were like gold."
—*Mary Silveira, Aide*

"No question about it,— Sil Conte, the
Congressman from Pittsfield, Massachusetts,
did more for our state than the Kennedys,
McCormack, Eddie Boland, Joe Moakley or
I did combined."
—*"Tip" O'Neill*
"All Politics is Local", 1993

A month after the election, Silvio's friends hosted a large dinner
to celebrate his victory. The guest speaker was the Republican Minority
leader, Joseph W. Martin, Jr., from North Attleboro, Massachusetts. He had
been in the U.S. House since 1925 and was held in high esteem and great
affection by both parties. He had been Speaker from 1947 to 1949 and from
1953 to 1955, when the Republicans had had a majority. He was pleased to
be honored because Silvio's election was one of the few Republican bright
spots across the county. Martin promised to help Silvio, who had pledged
to support Martin in his bid to retain his House leadership post.

Shortly after the election Corinne and Silvio, but mostly Corinne,
made an important decision. They decided to move the family to Washington. Corinne said she had had enough of Silvio being away all week in Boston for the last eight years and that the family would accompany him to
Washington. Silvio was afraid that the financial commitment would ruin
them but Corinne prevailed and they bought a home in Bethesda, Maryland where they lived for 32 years. The home not only benefitted the family

but also Silvio's political career. They transplanted the Conte hospitality to Washington and invited for dinner many members who were in Washington without their families. These dinners not only built friendships but also allowed Silvio to learn how members from other parts of the country and the opposing party felt about various issues.

Because he was Chairman of the Judiciary Committee in the Massachusetts Senate, Silvio hoped for a seat on the Judiciary Committee in the House—not a likely assignment for a freshman. He would have preferred Appropriations, but that was unheard of for a new member. When the 86th Congress met in January 1959 it was clear that the Republicans would choose a new leader. The loss of 47 seats, along with Martin's ill health and age, made the Republicans want new blood.

Martin's challenger was Charles Halleck of Indiana. This presented Silvio with a serious dilemma. If he supported Halleck, the obvious winner, he would be breaking his pledge to Martin; if he supported Martin he would alienate the new leadership before receiving his first committee assignment. He resolved this, voting as promised, for Martin. This gained the attention of his colleagues and further enhanced his standing with Martin, who despite his loss of the leadership post still commanded great affection, respect and clout. One result of the election was that the Appropriations Committee needed a New England Republican. The other potential candidate, Perkins Bass of New Hampshire, had not supported Martin, who specifically requested that Bass be denied assignment to that prestigious committee. This opened up a seat for Silvio on this powerful committee which drafts legislation for the money to be spent on each Federal program for each year. The seat on Appropriations where Silvio was to serve for 32 years gave him the ability to obtain funding for his own district along with influence with other members who needed help to get money for their programs and projects.

Silvio made an immediate impression upon the House. For one of his staff positions he retained Katherine Coupe, who had served with his predecessor for 12 years and was to serve with Silvio for another 25 years. She took him around the Capitol to introduce him to people she knew. She described him as so handsome and smartly dressed that one staffer told him, "You should not have run for Congress—you should have gone to Hollywood."

One day Silvio appeared in the office wearing a pink dress shirt and

Katherine said, "Mr. Conte, this is a very conservative place; they wear dark suits, white shirts and striped ties on the floor. They don't wear colored shirts." Silvio replied, "They do now." His experience in the Massachusetts legislature prepared him for both the procedures and the intrigue of the House. Two of his colleagues from Massachusetts, Thomas P. O'Neill, Jr. and Edward Boland, were old friends.

Silvio approached his Congressional duties at full speed and initiated the program he was to follow throughout his days in Congress. He devoted weekdays to legislative business and national affairs and the evenings, weekends and recesses to district and constituent matters. He seldom spent a weekend in Washington. At the end of the Congressional week he would drive six hours to Pittsfield to attend events throughout his large District. He responded to every constituent matter and saw that responses were promptly given and that necessary follow up work was done. These frenetic district visits strengthened the bond with his people who looked forward to seeing him at various functions. In Washington, after the Congress recessed for the night, he would spend a couple of hours answering constituent letters, following up requests and making calls back home.

Keeping in touch with half a million people in a large Congressional District is a mammoth task. Silvio always exerted extraordinary efforts to keep abreast of his constituency. In October 1960 at the end of his first term he said, "It is, I believe, the duty of a member of Congress, that the voice of the people always be heard." Throughout his years in Congress he remained faithful to this and spent much time in the District meeting with people and attending functions and parades. He tried to visit each of the towns and cities in the District at least once a year and once threatened to fire the staffer who suggested that meetings for some of the smaller towns could be combined. Some Thursdays he would call his Pittsfield office and ask that the papers and radio stations be notified that Friday he would hold office hours. The staff then knew that a long day was ahead. People would begin to line up at 7:00 or 7:30 a.m. for a start at 9:30 or 10:00 a.m. Throughout the morning, afternoon and into the evening everyone who came was seen. He would then expect that everything brought up by all these constituents would be handled to completion by the middle of the following week.

Silvio also went to great lengths to involve people in the process and mingle with them. In Washington he held a gigantic birthday party at the Capitol's Botanic Garden every November 9th. Hundreds of people were invited to eat the birds he had shot, fish he had caught, pasta prepared by family and staff and a huge cake sent down from the Pittsfield Rye Bakery. Guests would always include several busloads of friends from the District. In addition to a core of close supporters he would invite anyone he had met during the previous months. Back in the District he would hold a picnic at Mount Tom in late summer. Silvio and his people would provide hot dogs, hamburgers, popcorn, beer and soda and the public would be invited. Often over a thousand people would come. Silvio would walk around, talk with everyone and have his picture taken with his guests.

The biggest and most organized district event was his seminar in Washington held every other year. This started as an effort by the Westfield and Holyoke Chambers of Commerce to come to Washington and listen to some Federal officials talk about current matters. Over the years it grew as Silvio's position advanced. During the Reagan years, with Silvio as the senior Republican on the Appropriations Committee, he could put together an impressive gathering. For two days people from Western Massachusetts could not only listen to but also ask questions of the Speaker of the House, important Senators and Congressman, Cabinet Secretaries and other high ranking officials. In the early years only a small number came to Washington, but later it was advertised in the local papers and anyone who desired could attend the two-day session and an evening reception which Silvio hosted. About two weeks before the event the staff would panic and say no speakers will come, what are we going to do? Then Silvio would phone the prospective speakers who would always appear unless they were going to be on the other side of the globe. Several of them said, "I'm glad to be here for Sil, but because of his position even if I didn't want to, I'd probably be here anyway." The effect of these affairs was multiplied back home when many of those who attended were interviewed by local newspaper and TV reporters preparing news stories covering reactions to what had been heard in Washington.

These efforts not only benefitted Silvio at election time but also kept him aware of people's concerns. He was interested to know what they thought because it helped shape what he thought. During and before votes on controversial measures, he would frequently call his District offices to learn what opinions were being voiced.

Silvio spent much time reading mail from home. He would telephone a person with a particularly troubling problem and say, "This is bad, it shouldn't be; we'll get right into it." If someone wrote something with which he vigorously disagreed, he might phone to explain his position, never hesitant to express opposition to what had been written. He could be reached at home on the telephone and was accessible to anyone as he travelled the District. If approached on the street by someone saying, "Excuse me Congressman Conte", he would respond, "How ya doin'? Just call me Silvio."

From the first days in the Congress Silvio exerted extraordinary efforts on behalf of his district. He worked for new post offices, fought to save others from closing, obtained hundreds of grants for local community projects and assisted "the GE" in getting defense work. For his entire tenure in Congress he was involved in the struggle to control energy costs, especially high in New England. He fought quotas and import fees which served to increase fuel prices in Massachusetts. When the first oil shortages appeared in the early 1970s Silvio criticized President Nixon's policy, or more accurately, the lack of policy, saying, "Instead of a crash program to exploit our remaining energy resources, this country should be launching an Apollo-type program to discover and develop alternate sources of energy." For years Silvio served on the Small Business Committee because he believed it gave him the opportunity to channel resources in the form of loans to struggling enterprises in his distressed district. In 1974 he turned down the opportunity to become ranking Republican on the new Budget Committee in order to stay on the Small Business Committee.

In 1972, because of declining economic conditions, he sponsored an economic development conference at the University of Massachusetts in Amherst. Officials from Federal and State agencies provided information on jobs and economic assistance available from various programs. The first thing he did at the end of the conference was to set up follow through to assure that promises made at the conference were fulfilled.

Early 1979 greatly increased Silvio's clout for his district. In 1978 Silvio had no opponent. The key race for him and his district was in Michigan where Congressman Elford A. Cederberg lost. Cederberg was the ranking Republican on the Appropriations Committee and his defeat opened this position. Silvio was the heir apparent since he was next in seniority. Some conservative Republicans worked to block him from this important position because they believed him too liberal and too close to Democratic Speaker O'Neill. Normally the leadership positions are in place by early

January, but this took almost a month longer to resolve. When the vote was finally taken, Silvio got 92 out of 101 votes cast.

The rise to ranking member on Appropriations was a perfect fit. It gave him the opportunity to be involved in all aspects of Federal Spending programs. He could appoint the minority staff and make subcommittee assignments. He was involved in House-Senate conferences on all spending bills. He remained the ranking member on the Transportation Subcommittee and remained on Labor, Health, Education and Welfare, but he had to give up his ranking position on the Small Business Committee. An example of what he could do in this position which he held for 12 years came in his first week. The Carter administration requested a cut of $227 million in the Health and Education Appropriation, including $37 million for a children's facility at the National Institutes of Health (NIH). Silvio said "If you're going to take $35 Million away from little kids and pregnant mothers, I'll get it out of foreign aid for you." As the WASHINGTON POST said, "The money stayed in." While Silvio had to work within many constraints, this position gave him an overall view and enabled him to shift funds around to meet targets and caps and still protect his favorite programs. Despite being in the minority, Silvio managed to be tirelessly effective in this role. He worked indefatigably studying legislation. He knew the details of every piece of legislation and had a great sense of what members wanted and what would pass.

This new position helped Silvio with the great responsibility which he felt for the well-being of his people. He frequently returned to Washington overwhelmed by the problems described during his visits home. Whenever someone brought up retirement he would say that he felt a responsibility to stay and use his seniority and clout to bring back help to an area that had experienced long-term economic distress.

Silvio arranged many projects for his district. For years he had one staff member assigned solely to research Federal funding programs for the district. This staffer worked primarily with the local communities which grew from 84 in the 1950s to 95 in the 1980s to find Federal funds for schools, roads, bridges, water mains, sewers, police stations and fire houses. One who held this position said, "Silvio saw himself as a lifeline to a declining area." When necessary he played hardball politics with local projects. When the Air Force proposed to build transmitter towers in Hawley and Ashfield, a project which required taking many acres of wooded land, there was a great public outcry. Silvio did not get into the matter immediately but when he saw that the Federal government was trying to strong arm two small towns, he stepped in and got the project stopped. When criticized for being late in getting into this matter, he replied, "Why is it dead? Because they're writing letters? It's dead because I'm not going to put the money into the budget. That's why it's dead."

For years on the Appropriations Committee, Silvio had been involved in funding battles over the stockpiling of strategic materials not available in the United States. He was acutely aware of the costs of acquiring and storing materials as well as problems of availability. An effort to address this provided a large project in his District. In 1985 Silvio obtained $10 million in funding and in 1986 another $10 million for construction of a National Polymer Research Center at the University of Massachusetts in Amherst. This facility provided an expanded home for the UMASS Polymer Department which for two decades had done extensive research on synthetic materials, primarily plastics. The new facility's mission was enlarged to study and develop synthetics to replace strategic materials to reduce dependence upon imports and stockpiling.

In the heat of a battle with the Reagan administration, the Department of Agriculture decided to close a district office in Amherst. Silvio arranged to stop this as he told the papers, "You go back and tell and agricultural secretary that I'll take the wheels off his automobile." Silvio even resorted to one of his favorite targets for pork-barrel attacks—agricultural subsidies—when he secured a grant for $60,000 for the University of Massachusetts to study the production of Belgian endive as a local crop. Anything for the district. In 1985 when a West Springfield firm got a Federal contract to exterminate roaches in the Capitol, Silvio put on a white exterminator suit and went around the Capitol with them, making the newspapers all over the country.

For 24 years Silvio worked to clean up the Connecticut River so that salmon would return. His great dream began to be realized in 1985 when he secured $7 million for the Anadromous Fish Research Center in Turners Falls. This center would be a facility to study fish which migrate from the sea into rivers to spawn. Silvio got an additional $1 million for this center in 1987 and attended its dedication in 1990, when it was named the Conte Anadromous Fish Research Center. At the dedication he gave a speech and said how he loved the Greenfield-Turners Falls-Montague area, explaining that he almost settled there as a young lawyer.

In 1979 he began a battle against complex OMB regulations which were effectively stopping fuel assistance funds. "The impoverished and elderly will run out of heating oil, then must be refused service, then procure a voucher and go through a bureaucratic system to get the funds. By this time they may have frozen." Within six weeks the funds were available and Massachusetts received $15 million. This program grew into the LIHEAP program, Low Income Heating Energy Assistance Program, which Silvio championed every year until his death. His support for this program came directly from his people who told him how rising energy costs and harsh winters were a great hardship. Every year there were proposals to reduce or eliminate this program, which benefitted only a small section of the country. Silvio used every legislative device he knew to keep this alive. One year he even had Speaker O'Neill testify at the Appropriations hearing—a rare event.

At one subcommittee hearing Silvio sat and read the newspaper while several southerners and Californians discussed curtailing this program. Silvio kept reading until he finished the paper, looked up at Congressman Roybal, the chairman from California, and said, "You know Ed, I was in your district recently—what a wonderful climate you have—it's always warm. Then I went home to Pittsfield where it was five degrees below zero. I couldn't even let my dogs out." Without saying another word, he got up and left. The funding stayed in that year. By 1980 the program dropped the "H" so that warm areas of the country could get this money for air-conditioning—a change which Silvio denounced. "This amendment should be defeated. Under this amendment, Florida, Mr. Pepper, my good friend, I was surprised at him, because I bled with him for the poor, that rich state and that great, rich district of his—Miami—would get 147% more. This is unconscionable. People are driving down to Florida by the thousands. Why? To pick the oranges and grapefruits and live in that warm, sunny climate and they want to come up here and grab the money away from those freezing people in New England."

As the 1980s progressed, Silvio was better and better prepared for this annual battle. In 1988 when the Fuel Administrator proposed cutting the program Silvio sent a detailed questionnaire to the Administrator to determine the likely effects. When this was unsatisfactorily answered, Silvio had a hearing to determine the exact effect the cuts would have. When the administrator still could not answer adequately, Silvio had his own staff canvas all the states to determine the precise effect of this cut. Using this study and mobilizing his ranking position on Appropriations as well as being Chairman of the New England Congressional Caucus, he was able to get the House to pass the funding. When the Senate removed it from its bill Silvio worked to get it restored in conference. He explained his success after a 9 a.m. to 9 p.m. conference in his office. "I was stubborn and determined and held the conferees hostage." In a related fuel matter, Silvio, a participant in the 1990 Budget Summit, became livid with the inclusion of a two cents per gallon tax on home heating oil engineered by Senator Bentsen of Texas. All the New England papers reported Silvio saying,"I went up to Bentsen and said, "Hey, what the hell are you doing here? He started talking about people being unemployed in Texas. I don't know what the hell that's got to do with home heating oil." Silvio got the fuel tax on heating oil deleted.

BASEBALL COACH

"All his mighty team of elephants
and the trophy that they bore
You'll hear him boast forevermore
on the score 13 to 4."
—*Silvio O. Conte, 1984*
(Revision of Poe's "Ode to the Raven" to
"The Rantin' and the Ravin'")

*B*aseball took an early hold on Silvio's attention. He played with his buddies on a neighborhood ball field. A local team called the Wine A.C.'s played other teams from the surrounding area. A home game in Lakewood was a cause for great celebration in the Italian community, brought out en masse with their picnic feasts to cheer their team and have a good time.

Silvio's good friend Jake Barnini was the team mascot, wearing his uniform shirt with the wine bottle filling a glass. He arranged for Silvio to become one of the ballboys. The ballboys had a heavy responsibility—to retrieve balls gone astray as home runs or fouls. Baseballs were expensive and had to be brought back. Silvio never lost one.

At Boston College Silvio was on the football team which practiced at Fenway Park when the Boston Red Sox were away. This entitled Silvio to receive free passes to Red Sox games. Seeing these games kindled a lifelong love affair with the "Sox". Corinne and Silvio "lived and died with the Red Sox."

During 1962 Silvio also succeeded in his campaign to bring baseball to Congress. For years the Democrats and Republicans had an annual game, but Speaker Rayburn discontinued it in the 1950s because of many injuries and other problems. Silvio wanted it to build camaraderie among members and to challenge his competitive skills. It was not enough for him to fight in committee and on the floor all day, he wanted more in the evening. He promoted Congressional baseball the same way he did everything else—he persevered until everyone gave in. He became a Republican captain and played second base, later becoming Republican manager for 25 years. He worked the practices and the games as if they were the World Series. Republican practice began at 6:30 a.m. His people would be ready and they would not be injured. At a game Silvio paced the dugout, clad in his Boston Red Sox uniform and constantly smoking a big cigar. The first game saw the Republicans win 4 to 0 with Silvio saying, "The Democrats are soft on batting."

In 1970 Silvio could not play because he had chipped a bone in his hand during practice. He did extensive recruiting for the Republican team, saying, "If you can wing the ball at least a distance equal to the diagonal of your new desk; you can run the 40 in 4.5 (minutes, not seconds) and if you can stand the adulation that naturally is showered upon members of the Republican Congressional baseball team, then you are the type of barely-over-the-hill-athlete-statesman we need." Without being on the field he managed the team to a 7 to 3 victory.

Despite Silvio's efforts, 1971 was the last year for the Washington Senators baseball team. Silvio managed to combine agriculture and baseball into a single effort to try to save the team. In the midst of a heated debate about allowing sugar beet growers to obtain corn subsidies, Silvio proposed to give the Washington Senators an agricultural subsidy for not growing corn on their 3-1/2 acre ballfield. When criticized for this he pointed out that giving the money to the Senators was just as germane to the bill as giving sugar beet farmers the corn subsidy.

The approach of the 1978 Congressional baseball game had the press questioning Silvio about what pitchers he would use. Would he again go with "Wild Bill" Cohen from Maine, a candidate for the Senate? In an interview a few days before the game, Silvio said "He's good but wild as hell. He hit seven batters last year. I went out there and said, "Doggone it, Bill, you've lost too much control. You might hurt somebody. I stuck with him though." Speaker O'Neill threw out the first pitch and then went to a dinner at the White House. Silvio said, "He's putting the President ahead of us. I certainly wouldn't do that." Silvio's Republican team won again. His record was 14 wins for 17 annual games.

Silvio's loud voice was not confined to the ballfield. Tip O'Neill said, "It was bad enough that he won 14 years in a row, but he taunted us Democrats on the House floor both before and after each game." Before the 1985 game Silvio said at the beginning of one day's session, "It's my solemn duty today to report, Mr. Speaker, that I have learned that the Democratic Baseball Team is planning to depart to join the British Soccer Team. It is with a heavy heart that I report the sudden departure of my colleagues. This is not to say that I think that the Democratic ball team will do poorly in the British Soccer League. Their pitchers toss so low that the batters would be better off kicking the ball anyway."

In interviews he was asked about his work as House baseball manager and this provided good stories. Once when asked about injuries he said, "There weren't many but once a Democrat slid into first and there was blood all over. I ran over and he said 'I'm okay but my jaw hurts'. It turned out that he had broken his jaw. What a catastrophe—a politician at the start of a campaign with a broken jaw."

After 25 years Silvio finally gave up coaching because of a painful knee surgery, but not his interest in the sport. He proudly wore the Boston Red Sox ring which his beloved pal, Carl Yastrzemski, gave Silvio when "Yaz" retired from the Red Sox. Silvio often invited the Red Sox Players to the Capitol for lunch when they were playing in Washington against the Senators or later when they played in Baltimore.

He used the House floor to promote his beloved Red Sox when they neared a pennant or World Series, to applaud Carl Yazstremski when he won the Triple Crown or to denounce the umpire as "Looney Cooney" when he threw Roger Clemens out of the 1990 Red Sox-Oakland playoff game. To Silvio, the House was for serious business, but it could always spare a moment for baseball, sometimes to the dismay of other members.

GLOBAL CONGRESSMAN

"He saw the Congress as a perch to look out over
the country and the entire world."
—*Jim Fabiani, Aide*

*S*ilvio's first assignment in Congress was on the Foreign Operations Appropriations Subcommittee, responsible for the funding of Foreign Aid programs, always a source of controversy. Silvio dove into this with great energy and enthusiasm. He viewed Foreign Aid as the best way to fight "Godless Communism." He was sympathetic to people in need and favored using American funds to help people as an alternative to buying weapons. His strong anticommunist feelings arose from his father, who frequently told his children how great the country was, especially on the Fourth of July. The Foreign Operations Subcommittee was chaired by seven term Louisiana Congressman Otto Passman, who detested Foreign Aid. Silvio soon incurred Passman's wrath by taking the opposite position on almost everything.

In one Foreign Aid debate Silvio stated, "I have seen a proposition for $500,000 to eradicate water lilies get more attention than the written request of the President of the United States to provide $500 million for one of the most important programs in foreign relations." This enraged Passman because he had just arranged quietly, he thought, this water lily appropriation for the waterways in his own Louisiana district. For this embarrassment he refused to authorize Silvio to travel abroad to see first hand how and where Foreign Aid funds were being spent. At that time the Subcommittee had to approve travel expenditures. Silvio got around this with the help of his close friend, Bob Michel of Illinois, a fellow Republican on the

Appropriations Committee. Michel had entered Congress two years before Silvio, and was just ahead of him in committee seniority. Bob Michel served on the Agricultural Appropriations Subcommittee and was able to arrange for Silvio to travel through the help of his chairman, Jamie Whitten of Mississippi. They made many extensive foreign trips, including what Bob Michel later described as the "junket of all junkets," which began on the ocean liner UNITED STATES, leaving New York for Casablanca where they disembarked for a trip through all of Africa. For Silvio the trip was enhanced by travel with his good friend, because they got to visit the rural areas as well as the capitals. Silvio, an avid hunter and conservationist, was thrilled to see the many different animals in their natural habitats—lions, tigers, elephants, hyenas.

They saw apartheid first hand in South Africa where they visited Soweto as well as Capetown. The journey ended after seven weeks when the two Congressman met their wives in Milan. Seeing the problems that the emerging new African nations were facing as they struggled with independence strengthened Silvio's belief in foreign aid. His strong support endeared him to the Eisenhower administration, which favored an international outlook rather than the isolationism championed by many conservative Republicans and Southern Democrats.

Shortly after President Kennedy's death in 1963, another Foreign Aid battle arose. Subcommittee Chairman Passman, along with the conservative Republicans, led the charge to cut $800 million from the appropriation. Passman apologized for being Santa Claus and said much more should be cut. Silvio sided with the new President who was anxious not to have an early defeat from the Congress. The initial House bill passed with the cut but a compromise bill which came back from the Senate had some funds restored. Despite intense pleas from Republicans, especially Minority Leader Halleck, Silvio, along with his close friend, New Yorker John V. Lindsay, were the only two Republicans to vote in favor of the bill. Silvio answered Halleck's pleas by saying, "I can't sacrifice my convictions for you or anyone else, Charlie. This is important to the country and the free world." With this vote, once again for Silvio, conviction and practical politics came together. President Johnson was so pleased with Silvio's stalwart support in the face of both Republican and Democratic opposition that he frequently invited Corinne and Silvio to various White House events and always introduced Silvio as a "Great American." Shortly thereafter, Silvio was able to enlist the President's help in getting a substantial federal contract for GE in Pittsfield, then much in need of additional work.

Silvio gained nationwide prominence early in the summer of 1964. The House was in the process of considering the Foreign Aid Appropriations Bill from which Subcommittee Chairman Passman and most Republicans wanted to cut $447 million out of President Johnson's request. Silvio vigorously took up the President's international cause and cast the tie-breaking votes to get the bill out of both the subcommittee and the full committee, thereby killing Chairman Passman's reduction amendment. Passman was so enraged that he said on the House floor that those who voted with him were the best informed because they had attended the most committee hearings.

Silvio discarded his prepared speech and said, "The gentleman from Louisiana is asking the House to submit to a dastardly lie. I think I attended as many hearings as most of the members who signed the minority report. I agree that the attendance at the Subcommittee hearings was one of the poorest in Congress and I can understand the reason. Most members simply couldn't stand the tactics of the Chairman day after day. He not only asked the questions of the witnesses but insisted on answering them."

This vote made national headlines because Chairman Passman had never been defeated so dramatically before. In a profile, the *New York Times* said, "Few third term members have been able to become a burr under the saddle of the Democratic majority and a thorn in the side of his own party leadership." Silvio explained his stance very clearly. "It's not that I take pleasure in voting against my colleagues. It's only that I refuse to let somebody do my thinking for me, let alone tell what my convictions should be."

More irate than Passman were some of Silvio's Republican colleagues, especially Minority Leader Halleck, who took Silvio's defection to the President's cause as a personal affront. Some Republicans suggested that Silvio should go to the other side of the aisle and join the Democrats. To this he replied, "Why don't you put that question to my constituents?"

In 1965 Silvio began to question Foreign Aid appropriations and said that it was time for "a top to bottom overhaul." He wanted a prohibition on the use of these grants for the purchase of offensive weapons. Four years later he vigorously fought a $54.5 million Military Assistance Appropriation for fighter planes from Taiwan, "a big fat handout at the expense of the American taxpayer." Through extensive staff work he uncovered an unauthorized $157 million military material transfer to Taiwan. In 1976, Silvio opposed President Ford on aid for Angola, saying "I don't think any President can expect to channel some $50 million into a foreign war through the CIA without telling Congress and expect Congress to acquiesce in the whole thing."

In 1979, because Silvio had been so supportive of foreign assistance programs for his 20 years in Congress, the Carter Administration was concerned when he was to leave the Foreign Operations Subcommittee to become ranking member on the Appropriations Committee. Although of the opposing party, Silvio worked closely with the State Department in trying to fund those aid programs deemed crucial to U.S. interests. Secretary of State Vance called Silvio at home in Pittsfield to urge him to stay on this subcommittee. Silvio replied that he would still have a vote to take care of international needs and said, "At this moment I have a more immediate problem. As I am talking to you I am standing in two inches of water in the kitchen. My pipes froze and I thawed them out only too well just as you called." Silvio reported to the paper that Mr. Vance broke down in laughter and said, "It may have been the first belly laugh he's had in months, what with the breakdown in the Middle East peace talks and the awful mess with the Shah of Iran."

The position of Ranking Republican on the Appropriations Committee gave Silvio the opportunity to become, at times, an international congressman. In 1980, when massive earthquakes occurred in Italy, destroying many buildings around Eboli, Silvio arranged for reconstruction funds to provide food and medicine as well as rebuild schools, clinics and other vital structures.

Despite his increasing interest in domestic issues, Silvio still cared about Foreign Aid programs, especially those funded by the United Nations Development Program (UNDP) headed by his friend and former Massachusetts colleague, Bradford Morse. This agency funds food, technical and capital assistance to 150 nations, with the United States its largest financial supporter. In the early 1980s, as budget constraints tightened, Silvio was a significant player in keeping this funding stabilized and, at time, increased. For these accomplishments in 1983 he was given the Paul Hoffman Memorial Award for, as stated by his friend Brad Morse, "significant contribution to international development over the years, particularly the UNDP." Silvio gave a speech at the ceremony at United Nations Headquarters in

New York, attended by a large number of people from the district. Silvio summed up his outlook in the speech "We have come a long way from the days when every country ignored the problems of its neighbor."

Silvio's awareness of foreign developments was also sharpened by the many foreign trips which he took as ranking Republican on the Appropriations Committee. Silvio and Speaker O'Neill headed a number of Congressional delegations. In addition to many European trips, they made major journeys to China and Russia. Silvio was noted for being forthright and outspoken when meeting with heads of state. When foreign leaders would criticize the United States to the members of Congress, Silvio would not hesitate to give a sharp retort, especially to those leaders whose nations he had struggled to help with Appropriations. In a well publicized meeting with Soviet President Gorbachev, who made a number of references to homeless people in America, Silvio shot back suggesting a visit to Pittsfield to find the homeless. Once home, Silvio gave his assessment of the Russian leader to the press. "I think he'd be a good candidate for New York City. He's a sharp dresser. He's a smooth guy. He'll stare you down when he talks to you, eyeball to eyeball. He can go from very loud to purring like a kitten."

Silvio Conte as a law student at Boston College, 1947. *Conte Family Photograph*

Campaign blotter from 1952 Massachusetts State Senate Campaign. *Conte Family Photograph*

Silvio with Corinne and his parents, Lucia and Ottavio Conte, celebrate his first Congressional victory on Election Day, 1958. *Conte Family Photograph*

Congressman Conte with House Speaker Sam Rayburn, 1959. *Conte Family Photograph*

Congressman Conte with Republican Leader and former House Speaker Joseph W. Martin, Jr., 1959. *Conte Family Photograph*

President John F. Kennedy and Silvio aboard Coast Guard training ship, Eagle, 1961.
Official U.S. Coast Guard Photograph

President Lyndon B. Johnson signing Export-Import Bank bill with Congressman Conte attending, 1968. *White House Photograph*

President Richard M. Nixon meeting with Congressman Conte in early 1972. *White House Photograph*

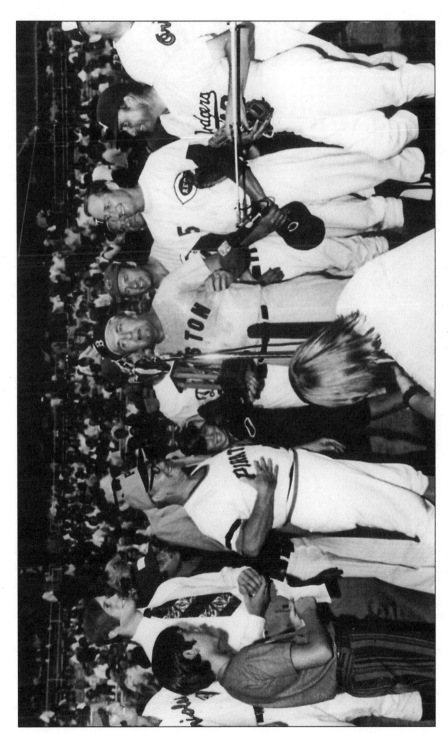

Silvio as manager of the House Republican baseball team accepting the winning trophy, 1970s. *Conte Family Photograph*

Silvio at his cottage on Onota Lake in Pittsfield preparing to go fishing, 1973. *Vincent D'Addario Photograph*

Silvio hunting with a young Primo, 1974. *Conte Family Photograph*

Congressman Conte with President Gerald Ford, 1975. *White House Photograph*

Silvio the Chef, 1979. *Vincent D'Addario Photograph*

Congressman Conte with President Carter, 1980. *White House Photograph*

INDEPENDENT

"I've been fiercely independent
—that's what they like about me."
—*Silvio O. Conte, 1982*
(Interview with Cokie Roberts)

T he only political label that fit Silvio was "Independent." Starting in the Massachusetts State Senate, Silvio plotted his own course, made his own decisions about what was right and held to those decisions with tenacity. This independence affected his relationship with his party. Often he went against the party line, especially when he took courageous stands ahead of most everyone else.

This independence made it difficult to categorize Silvio as liberal or conservative because he was both. Silvio's independence was strongly rooted in his Boston College education. The Jesuit tradition stressed independent and carefully reasoned thought. His Catholic family upbringing gave him a strong sense of right and wrong. He used these standards in making political decisions. While he was extreme in his devotion to family, church and the Congress, he was moderate and practical in his work.

In Silvio's first term in the Massachusetts Senate, he found his way into the limelight for an independent stand. Democratic Governor Dever wanted to increase the number of Superior Court Judges, in part because they were needed and, in part, to provide more good political jobs. In the State Senate the governor needed at least one Republican vote because the makeup of the Senate was 20 Republicans and 20 Democrats. Silvio's vote was seen as pivotal because he was the Republican least likely to vote the party line. The stakes were raised when it was intimated that Silvio could obtain a lifetime appointment to one of those judgeships—a position which would have more than doubled his pay. With this offer hanging over his head Silvio decided to vote "no" after driving all night from Pittsfield to Boston via New Hampshire and Southern Maine to ponder his decision. This began a long series of Conte votes of conscience. Later, in Silvio's State Senate career, a proposal arose to build a parking garage under the Boston Commons. Silvio was inclined to support this but when offered a campaign contribution to support the garage, he refused the money and voted "no".

When Silvio entered Congress, Sam Rayburn was Speaker of the House. He had been in the House for 46 years and he had served as Speaker for 14 of the previous 18 years. He was powerful and respected across the country. He maintained strong control over the House and was famous for his dictum, "If you want to get along, go along." This advice did not suit Silvio. Although he knew the legislative process and how to cooperate with fellow members, he did not accept the status quo. Had he followed Rayburn's advice, he would be working in "the GE" and never would have gotten to college or Congress.

Silvio went directly against this dictum in opposing both Democratic Subcommittee Chairman Passman and Republican colleagues in the battles over Foreign Aid programs. Silvio's next challenge of the status quo and his own party came in 1961, shortly after the inauguration of President Kennedy. Silvio knew President Kennedy well because he had often helped then U.S. Senator Kennedy while Silvio was serving in the Massachusetts Senate. Silvio agreed with many of the New Frontier's goals and favored Progressive legislation to move the country ahead. President Kennedy's legislative agenda was often stalled due to opposition in the Rules Committee. This committee, which sets the parameters for debate, debate time, amendments and so forth, would not report many bills to the floor so they simply died. The Rules Committee consisted of 12 members: eight Democrats and four Republicans. Two of the Democrats, Chairman Howard Smith of Virginia, in Congress since 1931, and William Colmer of Mississippi, in Congress since 1933, often voted with the Republicans.

After months of frustration, it was proposed that the Rules Committee be expanded to break this deadlock. Silvio was courted by the new President for his support in this expansion, opposed by conservative Democrats as well as most Republicans. In Silvio's own words, 25 years later: "In those days, young Congressmen kept their mouths shut and did what they were told to do. Taking a stand on this particular issue—voting my conscience—would cost dearly. I went to bed very late that evening, genuinely perplexed about what I would do on the House floor the next morning. I hardly slept at all and got up very early, still tossing the issue over and over in my mind. But on the walk from my office to the Capitol that morning, I stopped for some reason at the reflecting pool near the west entrance. The morning sun was bright, the air still, and I could see my reflection clearly in the shallow waters of the pool. What I saw went beyond the reflection in that pool to the very essence of my being. And I could see, at that moment, the answer to my quandary. Something about that moment, something spiritual, brought a new understanding, unleashed that inner strength that I had searched for. And I knew what I had to do—vote my conscience. I and a handful of Republicans voted to enlarge the Rules Committee and the rules were changed."

This stand endeared Silvio to the Kennedys, so much so that Senator Edward Kennedy remarked 30 years later, "Sil risked his own career when he voted against his party to expand the House Rules Committee and end its resistance to my brother's proposals." Not long afterward the President was visiting the University of Massachusetts and invited Silvio to return to Washington on his plane, but Silvio declined saying, "I have to go to Pittsfield to fix the floor in my house." To this the stunned President queried, "You don't actually do that work yourself?" to which Silvio replied, "Who the hell else do you think is going to do it?"

In 1963 Silvio again supported the administration on the Rules Committee membership increase. He voted in favor of a permanent increase. "It would have been much easier to vote against the enlargement. But my conscience tells me that I was sent here to debate the issues or vote on them myself and not to delegate the power of the First District to a group of six men on the Rules Committee." Again he angered his own party.

Silvio saw Congress as a forum to advance important national causes. In the early 1960s Silvio exhorted both parties to move ahead to correct rampant racial injustice. The year 1965 saw America catch up with Silvio on an issue he had long championed—civil rights. At the opening of Congress he joined a challenge to the seating of the Mississippi delegation because 400,000 people were denied the right to vote in that state. He and his friend and colleague, Edward Boland, were sent to Alabama by House Speaker McCormack to investigate the death of Reverend James Reeb of Boston who had been murdered in the civil rights struggle.

In Selma they met with Martin Luther King and walked in part of the March. "One of the objects of our mission is to show the local officials in Selma that Congress means business." The trip was cut short because of an important civil rights vote in the House. Upon his return to Washington Silvio reflected on his journey. "We are suffering from a grave illness and covered by a shame that is difficult to bear. Helmeted hounds of hate . . . neither honor nor right nor cloth of the church can prevent their brutality."

These stalwart civil rights views stemmed from his deep seated belief in equality and by his and his parents' personal experiences with discrimination as Italians. Many years later on a network special about Italian-Americans in public life he related, "As a young politician I found out what it meant to run as an Italian-American. I remember the first time I ran for the State Senate. I had a little blotter and it had a picture of myself, my wife and my three children. I didn't know too much about politics and it said on it "a statesman—not a politician." I went up to Williamstown and walked into a clothing store on a Saturday afternoon. The fella who owned the store shook my hand and I said my name is Silvio Conte and I'm running for the State Senate. He looked at me and said, "I'm glad you came in here. I pictured you as a dark greasy WOP."

Along with everyone else in public life in the late 1960s, Silvio was drawn into the Vietnam controversy. Although he had voted for the Gulf of Tonkin resolution, he grew increasingly uneasy about Vietnam. He charged Secretary of State Rusk and Secretary of Defense McNamara with being "less than candid". At home he was challenged by his two oldest daughters, Michelle and Sylvia, both enrolled at the University of Massachusetts and both strong war protestors. His district, strongly liberal, grew uneasy with Vietnam early on because it was home to nearly two dozen colleges and universities.

In August of 1967 Silvio attended an American Legion "Back the Boys" rally in Dalton and gave a long speech about the war calling for a bombing halt in North Vietnam, peace talks and construction of a barrier to provide a physical separation between the North and South. He also noted, "I cannot help but to reflect what we as people might have done, with proper planning and proper programs, to have prevented the calamitous rioting of recent weeks if we had not permitted ourselves to become enmeshed in this ever accelerating war on the Asian continent." His speech was politely and quietly received at this Legion gathering.

While his daughters thought that he was not moving fast enough in the anti-war arena, he was ahead of his very liberal district. Simultaneously with this speech he circulated a district wide poll which was answered by more than a thousand people and 70.6% still favored escalation of the war to defeat the enemy. As time passed he continued to call for peace talks and troop withdrawals. Eight months into the Nixon Administration he said the new President has had enough time to work on Vietnam and joined with Tip O'Neill and many other members in a resolution calling for expedited troop withdrawals.

Into the Ford years he continued to fight to end Vietnam spending. In 1974, he opposed funding saying "Peace should not cost more than war." He supported only enough funding to provide for an orderly removal of troops from Southeast Asia. Finally, in 1975 he was the key figure in killing the Ford administration's request for $722 million for Vietnam. "Fifty-six thousand American lives and $150 billion in American taxpayers' money for military operations is enough." When Saigon fell, President Ford attributed it, in large part, to the Conte led cut-off of aid to Vietnam; Silvio cheerfully accepted the "blame" for his role in ending the war.

Over the years Silvio took courageous stands on matters which he thought either needed attention or deserved a different approach. In 1978 he visited Cuba and, after seeing the hard times there, offered the opinion that the Cuban people would "come over to our side" if relations were normalized.

Offended by any discrimination, Silvio was upset by Nazi marches in Skokie, Illinois. From a rabbi in Holyoke, Silvio got the idea that the way to combat this sort of thing was to do something positive to balance the hatred. He proposed a resolution designating June 25, 1978 as Brotherhood Day. What was unique was that Silvio got this measure through the House and Senate in one day by getting half of the House members to sign his petition requesting it. President Carter signed the bill.

In 1983 he supported the administration-opposed sense of Congress Nuclear Freeze Resolution saying, "Whether you trust the Soviets or not, it's time we sit down and discuss this. It behooves us as a great nation to propose this. It is hard to know what the Russians are thinking, but we'll never know unless we try to find out." He also began to take the heat for other members on issues which they did not have the clout or the popularity back home to vigorously support.

One such measure was the Congressional pay raise. Silvio's home was now paid for, Corinne was selling real estate making more money than Silvio and their children were all long out of college. Silvio did not need the money. Yet he strongly campaigned for better Congressional pay because with inflation many members were not making ends meet supporting two homes and trying to educate college age children. To critics of this he simply said that Congressional pay needed to be more on a par with private industry, and that this was needed to keep and attract good people.

Shortly after the labor dispute which resulted in replacement of many air traffic controllers, the Reagan administration began hiring new postal employees at rates lower than existing employees were receiving. This violation of the postal workers' contract angered Silvio who got the House to pass an appropriations bill amendment prohibiting funding of a two-tier wage system for postal workers. This measure passed by more than 300 votes. When it moved to the House-Senate conference, Senate conferees attempted to kill this provision and replace it with a non-binding "sense of the Senate resolution." Silvio objected and House conferees declared that "true disagreement" existed, requiring that this provision be revoted in the House to determine whether support for it still existed. The revote received more votes than the first time and was widely publicized because the House had recently begun televising its proceedings on C-SPAN. The strength of the House vote and its accompanying publicity resulted in strong Senate acceptance of this provision. This legislation was eventually signed by President Reagan because it had enough votes to override veto in both the House and Senate and resulted in saving the postal workers from the same fate as the air traffic controllers. For the rest of his career Silvio remained a great hero to the postal workers and their union.

In mid-1989 the Congress wrestled extensively with another highly emotional issue—flag burning. Silvio did no grandstanding on this. He voted "no" on the bill to prohibit flag burning despite his own strong sense of patriotism, strong public sentiment in favor of the ban and particularly strong feelings on the part of many veterans who were close friends. Shortly after the vote Silvio came face to face with veterans' outrage.

Every summer the American Legion had an annual convention at the Hilton Hotel in Pittsfield—an affair that Silvio always attended. Some of his staff debated the political merits of his attending, given the hostile sentiment. When Silvio was advised of this, he replied, "I'm going. I always go." He got his pal Yaz to accompany him and walked to the podium as he was loudly booed. He said the same thing that he said on the House floor. "Tolerance is part of the fragile political spine of our country; tolerance of others of their differing backgrounds, religions, races, genders and ways of life. It is unpleasant at times, it is irksome at times, it is downright offensive at times. But it is the test of our greatness as a nation." The boos subsided and were replaced by some mild applause, not so much for a convincing argument but for an old friend who had the courage to stand up before a tough and hostile crowd.

Not all of Silvio's "independent" initiatives were completely serious. Irritated by Washington traffic jams, Silvio introduced a bill in 1963 to cut funding for Secret Service protection for the Vice President. "It's not that I'm against protecting the Vice President. Its just that I think it's time we started protecting the taxpayers as well."

Tip O'Neill related that Speaker McCormack sent him to see whether Conte had lost his mind. Silvio replied that he was "sick of LBJ's motorcades tying up traffic all the time. He's not so important that he can't come to work like the rest of us."

In 1976, Silvio launched an investigation by the Small Business Committee into a serious crisis which he discovered while gardening—a nationwide shortage of canning jar lids. When he could not get enough lids to can his produce, he began the investigation to learn the cause of the shortage. Soon sufficient lids began to appear and the crisis abated.

Silvio's independence was put to the test trying to moderate the Republican party, an effort that spanned his career. In 1963, Silvio was a leader of the Republican "Young Turks" who succeeded in replacing Republican Caucus Chairman, Charles Hoeven of Iowa, with Gerald Ford of Michigan. Silvio gained prominence at the 1964 Republican convention where he opposed Senator Goldwater for the nominee and where he lost a heated platform battle to include support for enforcement of Civil Rights, Federal Aid to Education, mass transit and the United Nations and denunciation of extremism, the Ku Klux Klan and the John Birch Society. When asked by the press why he would fight so hard for a lost cause, Silvio replied, "Even if we get clobbered, we ought to be in there raising hell to the end." His passion captivated many as he summed up his position. "The Republican Convention was dominated by haters, people who are for nothing, including the Republican party, and against everything; against Easterners, against the United Nations, against Labor, against civil liberties, against social security and all ethnic groups." Silvio took particular personal offense at prejudice in the platform against immigrants and ethnic groups.

Once home in Massachusetts, Silvio was widely acclaimed throughout the state for courageous actions in San Francisco. He joined a number of other liberal and moderate Republicans around the country who decided not to support Goldwater. His notoriety further increased when two members of the John Birch Society filed a one million dollar lawsuit against him for alleged slander at the convention. This matter went away because it could never be determined exactly what Silvio said that was slanderous.

After the 1964 election, Silvio took an active role in the Wednesday Group, a caucus of moderate Republicans working to move the party toward the center. Their immediate goal was to replace Halleck of Indiana as Minority Leader. Silvio was a key member in influencing other colleagues to support his good friend, Jerry Ford. The November election, which saw the Republicans lose 48 seats in the Goldwater debacle, made deposing Halleck easier because all he could say about the election was that the Republicans were lucky that they did not lose more. Some Republicans planned to remove Silvio from the Appropriations Committee for his failure to support the Goldwater candidacy. The leader of this movement, Iowa Congressman Jensen, was defeated in November so nothing came of this.

When Watergate became the primary national issue in 1973 and 1974, Silvio pleased neither the Republicans, the Democrats, nor many of his own constituents. He did not immediately take a stand. He had the Library of Congress research impeachment in American and British government going back several centuries and spent a month studying this. He was not to be pressured. He did his work and let the Judiciary Committee do its job. "My vote will be based on a respect for the Constitution and the rule of law rather than any partisan or personal loyalty."

As the 1976 Presidential convention began, Silvio remained in Washington working on legislation. The conservative Reagan forces managed to get him off of the platform committee. "I was here doing my job. We had important legislation and I couldn't leave. It's a hell of a note when they penalize me for doing my job as a Member of Congress."

When Silvio finally arrived at the convention he did attend a platform meeting. There he was photographed yawning by the press and the picture appeared in papers all over the country. Later he put this photo into words when he said, "I think it's asinine to say that any Republican officeholder is going to run on this platform. I'm not going to."

For Silvio, the Reagan era seemed to have great promise. The Republicans had control of both the White House and the Senate and hoped to take the House during the 1980s. Silvio agreed with much of the Reagan rhetoric that America needed new direction. He also was acutely aware of the need to do something about the mounting deficits. He knew the rising debt burden was harmful to the nation and felt that as a key Republican in the House he could add expertise, persuasion and clout to the reordering of spending priorities. Silvio saw an opportunity to get rid of wasteful programs and protect important education, environmental and health programs.

In the first Reagan year, 1981, Silvio took a good deal of criticism at home for his support of the President. He was a key player in the House in getting Reagan's "Recision" package approved. This legislation cancelled previously approved appropriations authority. In the middle of the fiscal year most agencies all of a sudden had less money to spend than they had thought.

Silvio felt that some work was needed to improve national defense. When Reagan proposed the first aid package to El Salvador of $5 million, Silvio was able to get this approved by the Appropriations Subcommittee despite heavy opposition, and then eventually saw it through to passage. This aroused great animosity in his own district.

The papers said that Conte is no longer a liberal but a Reagan conservative. In the extremely liberal eastern part of his district, Northampton, Holyoke, Amherst—there were demonstrations. His Holyoke office was the site of a sit-in by some 40 students demanding a personal meeting because they felt that a letter which he wrote to them explaining his position was unsatisfactory and a sellout to the President. This furor abated and later Silvio opposed further Contra aid. Although Silvio favored some modernization of defense, he did not want it done at the expense of gutting domestic programs.

Shortly after the "Recision" package the administration proposed an additional Defense Appropriation of $14 billion— completely wiping out the savings just realized. It was then that Reagan began to lose the full support of Silvio along with many other members who had taken so much heat for the recently-enacted cutbacks. Later Silvio identified this as the exact point when gridlock began. Many members retrenched and focused on their own programs and interests rather than supporting the President.

The arrival of the Stockman budget proposal further alienated Silvio and many others from the administration. David Stockman, a youthful Republican Congressman from Michigan, was appointed as the President's Budget Director. He and his staff proposed drastic cuts to eliminate or curtail many popular domestic programs such as Pell grants—college loans, Head Start, Amtrak, medical research, etc. All of this was abhorrent to Silvio who fought long and hard to establish and fund these programs. Silvio gave Stockman the nickname, "The Young Slasher," that would follow him through his career as Budget Director.

The Stockman Budget converted Silvio from a Reagan ally to a defender and protector of certain domestic programs. An attempt to enact part of this budget came when the new President told Silvio that he would veto a Supplemental Appropriations Bill which contained, among other items, funds to continue the student loan program. Silvio learned of this while having lunch at the Golden Lemon Restaurant in Holyoke. The waitress brought a telephone to Silvio's table and announced that President Reagan wanted to talk to him. The President told him that he would veto this bill to which Silvio replied, "Well good for you. Go ahead and veto the damn bill, but I'll tell you right now I'm going to fight you every step of the way." The President vetoed the bill, Silvio returned to Washington and led the successful charge to override the veto by persuading many members on both sides.

Silvio passionately believed in the need for Federal help to enable students to obtain higher education. He was deeply grateful for his chance to attend Boston College under the GI Bill and wanted that opportunity extended to all Americans. Beyond this specific issue, the Administration's proposals and actions contradicted Silvio's view of the Constitution. He was alarmed that the Executive Branch sought to take spending authority away from the Congress and said of the President, "I hope he learns a lesson. You just don't have 435 robots here in Congress that are going to vote in lock step." With this veto override, Silvio's independence became even stronger.

Yet, he was still needed by the administration. As ranking member of the Appropriations Committee, he was the one that Cabinet members and agency heads turned to to get funding for specific items and projects they wanted. As gridlock deepened, Silvio ended up in the middle of many battles. He could shape compromises that both the President and fellow members could accept because he always lived in the world of the possible. He always knew where the votes were and made many trips to the White House to explain this.

Of the 1984 Presidential Convention he said, "This convention will be boring. An old scarred veteran of platform committees, I know the platform ain't worth the paper its written on anymore." On opposing President Reagan Silvio said, "You're not only voting against your party, you're getting a lot of heat from the administration. The President will call you and the Vice President will call you and there are some very, very, very lonesome times."

Despite the increasingly adversarial nature of White House-Congressional relations, Silvio continued to be effective, and his detailed knowledge of all facets of spending legislation allowed him to be a key and sometimes the primary figure in fashioning compromises that would pass in Congress and avert a Presidential veto.

On a personal level, Silvio exerted every effort to maintain his independence, facilitated by his repeated electoral successes. In 1965, he gave up his law practice to devote his full efforts to Congress as well as to avoid any hint of conflict of interest. After Watergate, the press made extensive inquiries into the finances of members of Congress. Silvio made the required disclosures and said of his stock holdings, "I do not think about Friendly's Ice Cream every time I go to the House floor to vote." He defended the right to some privacy and flatly stated that Corinne's assets or income were of no public concern. He said, "I am more honest than a churchmouse" in a taped interview. When Silvio and an aide heard the tape, they asked to get it revised to as "honest as the day is long." When the reporter would not relent, Silvio said, "I suppose for the rest of my political days people are going to be asking how honest a churchmouse is and the answer, I guess, is that they are as honest as the day is quiet." This gave the reporter the only memorable quote.

Another criticism Silvio received was for sitting on the board of Berkshire Life Insurance, a position he held with great pride and would not relinquish. "It's prestigious. I thought it a hell of an honor for a poor Italian boy like me."

In his private life, Silvio was frugal, old-fashioned and conservative. As offended as he was by the right wing of the Republican party, he was also appalled by the rise of the protest movement. In a 1966 Brown

University speech, he decried "galloping nudists who carry signs with filthy words on them flouting every bond of decent society." What he thought was needed, "more restraint" and "more soap and water."

In a 1972 commencement speech he called for moderation and "tolerance for views that differ from our own." In a 1976 commencement address at North Adams High School he said, "I really become upset when I see people today—and unfortunately some are candidates for office—waving the bloody shirt of Vietnam or the soiled shirt of Watergate in misguided attempts to incite hatred, mistrust and vindictiveness." He urged students not to "drain their vitality in anger."

At another commencement address the following year at Greenfield Community College, he told the students, "A person who thinks his school years are the best is a person who has a wasted life. No one who strives for self-betterment looks backward to find the best years of his life. To such a person the best years are always now and there are better years ahead."

All these opinions sounded more like a conservative Republican of the "Silent Majority" than a liberal, activist Congressman.

WITH FAMILY AND FRIENDS

"The family is everything"
—*Silvio O. Conte*

Silvio's friends frequently spoke of the dimension that he added to their lives. He was always upbeat, moving ahead, full of fun and ready with new jokes. Knowing Silvio was an adventure— no one knew when he would call unless one was a baker who had to get up at 3:30 a.m.—then it was certain that Silvio would call after 11 at night.

Arnie Robins, proprietor of Silvio's beloved Pittsfield Rye Bakery, recalls a midnight request from Silvio to pick him up in Boston the next day so Silvio could ride in Arnie's new car. After repeated protests, Arnie finally agreed to meet Silvio at noon after most of the morning's baking would be completed. At the appointed spot Arnie found Silvio, who jumped in his car and said, "We have to make a quick stop." After a short ride, Silvio told Arnie to park. "We're going to lunch." Arnie protested that he could not go dressed in his bakers clothes covered with flour, but Silvio said, "C'mon, don't worry about it. You gotta eat before we go back to Pittsfield," as Silvio led him to the head table at the governor's inaugural luncheon.

Another source of entertainment was attending horse races. At home he would gather up some friends and speed up the back roads to Saratoga. On the way home Silvio would stop and buy fresh corn and steaks and grill them at 11:00 at night. "No, we won't stop for dinner. I'll do the cookin'." What Silvio did was done with intense enthusiasm—even running out of a wedding reception to check on some Saturday afternoon horse race results.

Leisure time was handled with the same intensity as everything else. A typical day off in Pittsfield might start with a home project such as re-building the bocce court in his yard. Early in the morning he, along with his son John, would set to work, dressed in old clothes and sneakers, and work until four or five in the afternoon. At the completion of the day's work Silvio would clean up and start to prepare dinner. He would usually do much of the cooking for 15 to 20 family and friends he was anxious to see. After a couple of hours of polenta, pasta, risotto, steaks or whatever he was featuring that day, the folks would then play cards until 1 or 2 a.m.

Despite Silvio's intense interest in politics, public matters were seldom discussed with friends. Silvio might answer a question or two or tell a story, but frequently would say to his family and close friends, "I'm glad to see you so I can get away from all that." Another favorite pastime was playing bocce with his old Pittsfield friends. These games, although between old friends, were highly competitive and frequently loud, the volume fueled by the coffee laced with grappa consumed by the players.

Golf was another activity Silvio enjoyed both in Pittsfield and Washington. At home he played with a number of his old friends who often taunted him about his poor playing. Silvio frequently told them, "I get more respect from the President of the United States than from you guys." The quality of his playing did not detract from his enjoyment or intensity. Jack Martin remembers that he would jump three feet in the air after winning a nickel bet for making a putt. These Pittsfield pals would not be surprised to get a Friday afternoon call from Nan, the manager of his Pittsfield office, urging them to take him golfing so the staff could get some work done.

In Washington he could play in the early morning before the Congress began its work. His friend, Bob Giaimo, relates that he brought the same intensity to his golf game as he did to the legislative process. Despite being known as a poor golfer, he sometimes was so determined that he willed the ball to go where he wanted. In an early morning game, Silvio hit the ball into water, removed his shoes and socks and walked into the pool to play it. When Silvio, splashed with mud and water, was asked why he didn't just take a stroke and play on, he replied, "That's where I hit it and that's where I'll play it."

Occasionally Silvio would get the idea to undertake a major home improvement project. All of a sudden he would decide to remodel, re-do the roof, build something, or re-lay a floor. The first person to call would be his brother-in-law, Joe, a master carpenter who would say to him, "Oscar (as in the Odd Couple), how the hell are you going to do that, you don't have the right tools and you don't have enough time? You're just going to make a mess." Silvio would start and then have to rush off to Washington. If Joe wasn't already on the job, Silvio would have the office call and tell him that "there were a few loose ends" to pick up for the project and could he run over and take a look. Sometimes Joe would be called to come to Washington to lend a hand with a house project there. "Bring Betty, too, she can make risotto while you're helping me." The Washington house jobs got scaled back after Joe fell off the roof.

Vacations for the Contes were well executed events. Silvio would make the elaborate plans. Trips to Italy with his family were mapped out well ahead of time. Silvio decided where to go and then contacted those he knew in the areas to be visited and arranged to meet them. Every trip became a reunion. One of his favorite spots was Disney World where, Michelle and Corinne said, he planned their trek by carefully marking his map with the path to be followed. His family said he was more excited about going there than anyone else because he had the opportunity to relive what he had missed growing up in the Depression.

The struggling Conte family could not take vacations in the 1930s. They had neither the time or the resources. Silvio had some of his childhood while serving in Congress, as Michelle said, "He was just like a little kid."

Whenever the Contes arrived at the place they would stay, Silvio would head right for the kitchen to get a large pot. Once it was filled with water, he would reach for his brief case filled with deer bones to toss into the pot to make a stock for soups he would prepare during their stay. Frequently vacations were combined with other work: A visit to an area to be set aside as a wildlife refuge, a speech at a college which he had helped, a tour around a fellow member's district to help with an upcoming campaign.

"Disney ought to come see us if he wants some good dog stories for the movies," Silvio would say to Corinne about their adventures and misadventures with dogs. The Contes had many different dogs who were either gifts to the family or just wandered in. One of the most memorable was Gus, a weimaraner, who was beloved by Corinne and the kids. But Silvio did not like Gus because he was wild and always in trouble. One Christmas Corinne and Silvio came home with a ham, several boxes of chocolates and some wrapped gifts including Corinne's new leopard coat. For a short while they were out and Gus ate the ham, most of the chocolates, chewed the corners of the gift packages and ate holes in the leopard coat. When they returned Silvio was livid and said, "I'm going to get a gun and kill him—he ruins everything." Corinne replied, "No you aren't. He's my dog and I love him— more than the leopard coat—he only did this because he's lonely." Gus lived for many more Christmases.

Gus was also an unwelcome party guest. One time the Italian Ambassador and his wife were invited to dinner at the Contes' Washington home. Corinne prepared several platters of elaborate hors d'oeuvres, all of which Gus ate while they were upstairs getting dressed. Silvio was enraged but Corinne said, "Don't worry, I have plenty more." Then Gus would get lonely in the house and often jump through the patio screens to get outside. This happened so many times that whenever Silvio went to the local hardware store he was greeted with, "Well, Congressman, how many yards of screen do you need today?"

In 1973 Silvio decided he would get his own dog for bird hunting. He picked a male Brittany Spaniel and named him Primo. Primo soon became Silvio's best friend. He not only went hunting with Silvio, but everywhere else, too. "Primo has slept in more motels than George Washington." In Washington Primo was supposed to sleep in a backyard house with a tin roof, but frequently slept outside Silvio's bedroom by the door keeping watch. Not only was Primo his pal but also his confidante. Sometimes Nan in the Pittsfield office would ask how he was going to Washington and he would reply, "Primo and I will take the Jeep. I'll get a few cigars and Primo and I will talk all the way to Washington. I tell him all my problems and when he looks at me with those big brown eyes, I'll know what to do." Nan would reply that the Jeep was old and might not make it, besides, you're an important Congressman. What if people see you talking to a dog? Silvio always replied, "We're going and we'll have a good time." Primo was ever present and his white fur was everywhere. Corinne or one of his children had to brush off Silvio's dark suits before he went out. They would say, "You like to think of yourself as the Education or Environmental Congressman, but what you really are is the Dog-Hair Congressman!" Primo spent 13 years with Silvio and finally died in Washington. Silvio brought him back to Pittsfield in a steamer trunk wrapped in a quilt his mother had made. He was buried in the yard at their house at Onota Lake. Primo's grave is marked with a granite stone with his name, dates and "My Faithful Pal, Congressman Silvio O. Conte." Silvio sobbed and sobbed for days. He later got another Brittany whom he named Jaz, but he was not a great success for hunting because he ran away whenever he heard gunfire.

Frugality was a well-known Conte trait, another result of growing up in the Depression, a time when every penny was watched. It was reinforced by the belief, imparted by his parents, that credit spending was not good. This carried over to the time when he became financially comfortable. It took Corinne 20 years to convince him to expand the kitchen and the upstairs of their Pittsfield Cottage so that it could accommodate their four children and their families. The Contes lived in the same house in Washington from the time Silvio entered the Congress until he died. He took extreme pride in the fact that his clothing came from Filene's Basement in Boston. Their famous sales produced many of his outfits, on many occasions mismatched with plaids, stripes and clashing colors. He loved to tell people how many years he could get out of a suit, yet he could appear very distinguished if he chose. His sister, Betty, did his shirts from his graduation from college until mid-way into his Congressional career. Not only did she wash, starch and iron them, but also she removed and reversed the collars and French cuffs to extend their lives. This continued until one day when Silvio brought Betty two particularly decrepit shirts which she discarded. When Silvio asked if she had taken care of them, Betty replied, "I sure did, I threw them out, they're not even worth saving for dust rags." Silvio said, "They were two of my favorite shirts", to which Betty replied, "Every shirt is your favorite shirt, it's time to buy some new ones."

A number of aides encountered Silvio's ire when they went to fill his car with gas and failed to get the lowest price. Once he called the Washington office from Alaska to tell them to buy some hams at Giant Foods for an upcoming party because he had just read in the paper that there was a big sale. The half glasses which he wore part way down his nose for reading cost $3.95 per pair and he had several dozen pairs. He said there was no need to spend more because with the prescription number the proper glasses could be bought in any drug store.

But frugality was cast aside for the family Christmas. When in the Senate in Boston, he had a station wagon he filled with toys for his children. The limit on his spending was how much he could fit into the car. Once home he could go out and buy clothing and jewelry for Corinne. He adored Christmas and everything about it and expense was not spared. Christmas was always spent in Pittsfield with all the family. Because the Conte cottage had a high ceiling in the family room it had to have the biggest Christmas tree in Berkshire County. Silvio's old pal, Jake, was challenged each year to find one bigger and better than the year before. In the later years, major logistic problems were created figuring out how to get the tree into the house and how to set it up. From the early Senate days Silvio started dressing up as Santa to please the little children, both his own and their cousins. He had all his family and many friends come over on Christmas and told his children and grandchildren of his boyhood days when he only got an orange and a silver dollar. He stressed to the children and grandchildren how he loved those days because of the family.

One year his grandsons, Jason and Ryan, wanted an All Terrain Vehicle. Silvio took a huge ATV box and wrapped it with a big red bow. Inside were two dictionaries which he told the crestfallen boys would be of great benefit to their education. Once they became occupied with other gifts, he slipped out the back door and drove around to the front window on a shiny, new, bright red ATV, grinning broadly and puffing on his big cigar, even more delighted with the surprise than his grandsons. His frugality and gruff exterior masked a big heart and many times, a soft touch, especially for kids and those in need. The same aides who were berated for spending a penny a gallon too much for gas knew that he was always there in time of need and many saw him break down and cry when they finally told him it was time to move on to other jobs.

Relaxation was intense and competitive for Silvio. He enjoyed both fishing and hunting with his pals whenever possible. He fished for trout, bass, rockfish, bonefish, tarpon and salmon, from his own backyard, on Onota Lake in Pittsfield to the Chesapeake Bay in Virginia, South Carolina, and The Florida Keys, New Brunswick, Manitoba and Alaska. His competitiveness and intense ambition to get the best catch were always evident, even at home. Longtime friend Jack Martin recalls Silvio coming home one warm afternoon and asking him to go on a boat ride to try to catch some trout. Silvio was in the midst of describing some complex legislation when he stopped in mid-sentence because he spotted a boy pulling in some fish. He promptly went over and hollered "Hey, kid, what bait are you using?" After getting the information they resumed fishing and their legislative discussion. From Washington he would often take quick trips to the Eastern Shore of Maryland for a few hours. He would go to Manitoba sometimes to fish in pristine, unsettled wooded areas. Once he tried to get Tip O'Neill to go with him, telling Tip how beautiful and unspoiled it was. Finally Tip asked "Can you get all the TV channels up there?" To this Silvio replied no. Tip said, "Can't go. How can I keep in touch with what's going on?"

Every Spring Silvio had a fishing derby at home where about 75 friends, both from home and Washington, were invited to breakfast, a day of fishing and a big dinner in the afternoon. Silvio's other regular fishing expedition was his annual August trip to Kodiak, Alaska. For this journey he would take a few friends to fish for salmon for two weeks. He had to have enough fish for Labor Day—"My Alaska Salmon Party"—also held at home in Pittsfield with Silvio doing much of the work preparing thick salmon steaks. Silvio loved to fly over the countryside to look at the lakes and unspoiled country. He was always on the lookout for bears because they knew where the salmon were. His fishing pals all recall his exuberance and delight at being back in Alaska, especially if he caught the most salmon.

Considerable preparation was required for the Alaska trip because Silvio brought the food, venison, fresh tomatoes and other vegetables from his garden and herbs—fresh basil, rosemary. He did much of the cooking, giving an Italian flavor to his cuisine. Sometimes, because time was short, Silvio and his party would set out in bad weather. Because of the vastness of Alaska, some fishing trips required a plane, such as to Karluk Lake, almost 100 miles across Kodiak Island. On one trip a storm came up with blinding rain, lightning and heavy seas on the lakes below, necessitating flying 50 feet off the ground. One of his pals recalls looking back into the passenger cabin and seeing Silvio with his eyes closed, crossing himself. Soon the weather cleared and a safe landing was made. Later at dinner Silvio's friend Jay, seeing that Silvio was still a little out of sorts, asked how he enjoyed the flight. Silvio replied, "I made peace with my maker too soon." No one ever found out what he promised.

Silvio's other passion was hunting, which he enjoyed whenever he could. At home he belonged to a small sport club just over the Massachusetts line in Austerlitz, New York. He would frequently hunt there hoping to get some pheasant or quail for which the family had a number of treasured Italian recipes. Joining Silvio on hunting trips for about a dozen years was Primo, who would retrieve Silvio's birds and flush them out of the brush. Primo was highly travelled both at home and around Maryland, Virginia, Pennsylvania, Alabama, Texas and West Virginia. Anyone who invited Silvio had to expect Primo, too. Hunting on the Eastern Shore or in Virginia provided Silvio with a quick escape from the Capitol, sometimes for a couple of hours, other times for the whole day. On a Saturday he would hunt geese in the morning and deer in the afternoon. One hunting pal was Father Bill George, who frequently said Mass for Silvio and others on trips. Father George, a close family friend, said that no matter where he went or how remote the spot, Silvio either went to church or attended Mass and Communion at his camp site.

When hunting with Silvio one had to be quick because he was, contrary to Tip O'Neill's eulogy in which he said Silvio could not hit a barn, a good shot and a quick shot. Silvio's guests had to be careful not to be too good or too quick and outshoot him because this would aggravate him. "I didn't bring you out here to shoot all my birds." On occasion, especially during the Reagan years, some administration members might be hunting with Silvio to try to persuade him to help on some pending piece of legislation. Silvio would either tell them that he was outdoors to relax and hunt or make them tromp around all day long before he would let a legislative matter even be mentioned.

Close to his love of hunting was Silvio's interest in firearms. He was a collector of weapons and enjoyed having good equipment. On a trip to Italy with a Congressional delegation, Silvio left the group and, at his own expense, made a side trip to Brescia in order to get a particular type of shotgun at the Beretta factory. When Tip O'Neill saw it, he inquired about its cost and said "What the hell do you need that for? They probably won't let us back into the country." To this Silvio replied, "I always wanted one of these. It was a hell of a good deal." Just before boarding the plane to return home, Dante Fascell noticed the same shotgun for sale at a base exchange but no one ever found out whether Silvio paid more or less at the factory.

In the last months of his life, hunting on the Eastern Shore or in Virginia was one of Silvio's only sources of recreation because he had to be near Washington for chemotherapy treatments for the prostate cancer first operated on in 1987. He would go out with one or more of his pals and try to get a deer. He became obsessed with the failure to get one, believing that this failure was an omen meaning he would die. Each trip became more intense as Father George, Jim Desmond and Claude Hobbs took him all over the area. Finally, one day on the Eastern Shore, Silvio got an eight-point buck—the best one he ever shot, so he said. This deer, as many others he shot, was carefully dressed, cooked and served to his friends by Silvio himself.

Not often are the careers of two politicians so closely linked for so long a time as were those of Silvio Conte and Tip O'Neill. Seldom does that bond stretch to members of opposing parties. From the early 1950s in the Massachusetts legislature until the end, Silvio and "Tip" were "pals" as well as close allies.

The rise of Tip O'Neill to House Speaker in 1977 further strengthened the O'Neill-Conte bond. Mrs. O'Neill moved from Cambridge to Washington and Corinne, who was working as a real estate agent, found them a condominium. This friendship went beyond politics and Massachusetts. The O'Neills had dinner and played bridge with the Contes almost every week. Silvio said "Tip's my dear and beloved friend who loves my cookin', but he's a lousy bridge player." To this Tip replied, "My favorite dish is Flora's gnocchi and Sil always overbids in bridge because he wants to play every hand." Flora, a long-time family friend from Pittsfield, also often spent time with the Contes.

Their friendship both on and off the Hill transcended party politics. Silvio worked closely with the Speaker on many matters, especially those affecting New England. Tip relied on Silvio to watch certain legislation for him and Tip said that Silvio was one of the most skillful legislators ever to come to Congress. "He knew what everyone was for. He knew what everyone was against and most important, he knew when those who opposed his programs would be out of town." Silvio said of the Speaker, "He drove me crazy on the Appropriations Committee. He'd call me nearly every other day. Get this money in. Get that money in." When there were Congressional trips abroad, the Speaker would designate the members to travel when there were visits with Heads of State. Nearly always the Speaker arranged for Silvio and, if possible, Corinne also to go. Tip enjoyed Silvio's company and the entertainment that he provided and appreciated the extraordinary briefing and preparatory work done by Silvio's staff.

Silvio was welcome at many Democratic gatherings and was one of the principal roasters of the Speaker at a 1978 Democratic fundraiser. He said, "Tip received a lot of credit for changing the House Rules to permit Republicans to hire one-third of the committee staffs. The press reported that he did this out of a sense of justice and fair play. Baloney. I won that reform from Tip in a gin rummy game."

They worked well together because they shared common values and ideas. They both came from immigrant backgrounds and believed that the purpose of government was to improve the lives of its people—specifically in education, health, environment and infrastructure. Their political styles were similar. They were both close to their constituencies; they were both outgoing and personable; and they both loved to tell stories and jokes, eat and have a good time.

TRANSPORTATION CONGRESSMAN

"He should take the train to New York City
and meet the people who use it."
—*Silvio O. Conte, 1984*
(On Budget Director, Davis Stockman's plan
to eliminate Amtrak.)

*I*n 1969 Silvio became the Ranking Republication on the Transportation Appropriations Subcommittee and became heavily involved in securing funding for the nation's transportation projects. The year 1970 saw the enactment of legislation creating Amtrak, America's passenger railroad. Silvio worked diligently both in committee and on the floor to see that funding legislation was passed so that Amtrak could start operating in 1971. This began Silvio's long, fervent support both for Amtrak and other rail passenger and freight programs. Four years later he played a key role in getting the Boston-Albany-Chicago train running again, restoring service to Pittsfield.

He worked to overcome Democratic leadership opposition to funding for the Washington Metro. This project was favored by the Senate, President Nixon and many House members but was being stalled in favor of a Washington, D.C. bridge and highway project supported by the Democratic leadership of the Appropriations Subcommittee. Working with Connecticut Congressman Robert Giaimo, Silvio helped persuade enough members to get funding legislation to the floor and finally approved. Conte was asked why he would fight so hard and expend so much political effort for something so distant from his district. The answer lay in his belief that mass transit was a necessary environmental and economic benefit. His support followed his efforts to include mass transit in the 1964 Republican platform.

On the negative side he fought funding for the Supersonic Transport (SST) with the belief that the benefits of extremely high speed aircraft did not justify the federal investment. In both 1970 and 1971 funding was initially killed and then substantially restored, causing Silvio to remark, "The Republican leadership did so much arm twisting that some congressmen won't be able to lift a cocktail glass for at least a month."

Transportation also played a personal role in Silvio's life. In 1970 he purchased the automobile which was to be his trademark for the rest of his life—the 1970 bright red Pontiac GTO convertible known as "The Judge." Because of his long weekend trips to Pittsfield, he frequently had to buy new cars. In spite of his strong conservation sympathies he loved large fast cars. Many of his friends from Pittsfield recollect terrifying, record breaking trips to Washington in this red missile. He needed some convincing from the dealer who told him he deserved it. Silvio was worried that it was too ostentatious. He always exerted particular efforts to avoid criticism about his personal way of life, greatly aided by his extreme frugality. He did make the purchase for less than $4,000.00 and grew to love the car. It was in campaigns, newsclips, parades—many people in Washington and Western Massachusetts fondly remember Silvio charging around in "The Judge" with the top down—always smoking a big cigar.

Near the end of his career he was in an automobile accident enroute to his office in Washington when he hit a wall and the car caught on fire. He was trapped but soon rescued. "The Judge" was off the road for a year. It cost double the original purchase price to repair. This story resulted in an article in *Sports Car Illustrated*, describing Silvio's long love of The Judge. "One of these factory hot rods did not end up with a hormonally distorted adolescent . . so if you happen to be visiting the Nation's Capitol, gawking at the monuments, keep an eye out for a silver haired congressman in a bright red Judge convertible with a Massachusetts No. 1 congressional license plate. And unless you are in a Callaway Corvette be prepared to get blown away at the next light on Pennsylvania Avenue. The man likes to drive." Corinne recollects a trip to Italy when they visited a race course where they met Mario Andretti. After Silvio got to drive his car he told the famous race driver that if he had not gone to Congress he would have been a race car driver.

By the early 1970s the railroad network in the Northeast was in collapse. Some 6,800 track miles of the Penn Central Railroad were designated sub-standard and many industrial branch lines, some in Silvio's District, were threatened with extinction. This crisis led to the enactment of the Regional Rail Reorganization Act of 1974. Silvio, as ranking member on the Transportation Appropriations Subcommittee, oversaw the day-by-day planning as he poured over maps and charts to decide which lines would be retained once the Conrail system was created in April 1976. From 1973 to 1981 Silvio worked tirelessly to obtain funding for rehabilitation of the rail lines in the Northeast. He believed that the viability of rail service was intimately connected to the economic wellbeing of the region. He worked to get rail rehabilitation funds attached to transportation bills, job bills, public works bills, etc. Silvio received some criticism for supporting pork barrel legislation but he continued to be the key supporter for rehabilitation funds. These efforts ultimately produced substantial public benefit. Nearly half of the funds advanced were eventually paid back to the government when Conrail was sold in 1987. This line became profitable and began to pay federal corporate income tax, returning additional funds to the Treasury. And finally, the Northeast rail system became healthy and viable, a condition which had not existed since World War I. For the rest of his tenure he continued to be the champion of railroad rehabilitation throughout the country.

Also under the Department of Transportation was another Silvio favorite, the Coast Guard. Every year during the 1980s Silvio fought hard for Coast Guard funding. He had admired the Coast Guard ever since he was in the Navy Seabees and was involved with a joint Navy-Coast Guard operation. As Silvio said in opposing a cut in Coast Guard funding,

"If any agency in the Federal government is suffering today from lack of funds it is the Coast Guard of the United States. This Congress stands up here and anytime anybody gets a bellyache they put in a piece of legislation and they get it passed and they give the Coast Guard missions they never had before—fisheries, enforcement, drug interdiction, pollution enforcement. They never had that. A 5% cut would be a disaster. They need this money desperately. Where are you going to cut this 5%? The Coast Guard is at the bare bones. Unfortunately they don't have any big defense contractors who fight in their behalf up here. There are some of us up here who feel for the Coast Guard even though you couldn't get a canoe up my Housatonic River. I believe in the Coast Guard."

For several years Silvio tried to get legislation passed to levy an annual fee on recreational boaters to help support the Coast Guard. At one hearing for this, Silvio showed up wearing white pants, a captain's hat with gold braid and a sport jacket decorated with yachting flags of every type and color. On the floor he explained his program:

"The other $100 million would have been raised from the modest fee of less than $20 per year—what they pay, these fat cats and the yacht owners, for a bottle of scotch, to be paid every year by recreational boaters who use waters under Coast Guard jurisdiction. With about 6 million recreational boaters in this category it would take a fee of less than $18 per year to raise $100 million. We had a hearing on this last June by the Merchant Marine Subcommittee on Coast Guard. The general reaction, as I recall, was that the members would oppose me with an open mind. Isn't that great. I regret that attitude. The selfish interests of a small minority of boat owners are going to result in a tremendous loss of Coast Guard service. I think it's incredible that boaters of this country would refuse to pay $18 a year— a lousy $18 a year to help pay for Coast Guard Search and Rescue missions. I wish the Rules of the House would let me sing my little song and if they did it would go something like this:

Row, row, row my boat gently up the stream.
But if you try to make me pay, I'll throw a fit and scream.
Tow, tow, tow my boat through the surf to shore.
So what if I don't pay my share, the others can pay more.

I hope that after hearing that the boaters would change their tune and sing this song:

Search, search, search for me when I am overdue.
The Coast Guard needs these user fees to pull us safely through.
Tow, tow, tow my boat, I'll pay that user fee.
Because when I really need it the Coast Guard is there for me."

Silvio meeting with President Ronald Reagan and Vice President George Bush, 1981. *White House Photograph*

Silvio salmon fishing in Alaska, 1984. *Conte Family Photograph*

Silvio "Roachbusting" in the Capitol, 1985. *Holyoke Transcript-Telegraph photograph*

Congressman Conte, dressed as a yachtsman, testifying before a Congressional Subcommittee in favor of the Coast Guard "user" fee, 1985. *Kenneth Garrett Photograph*

Congressman Conte in Moscow with Soviet General Secretary Gorbachev, 1985. *Conte Family Photograph*

Silvio and Vice President George Bush attending Speaker "Tip" O'Neill's St. Patrick's Day luncheon on Capitol Hill, mid-1980's. *Conte Family Photograph,*

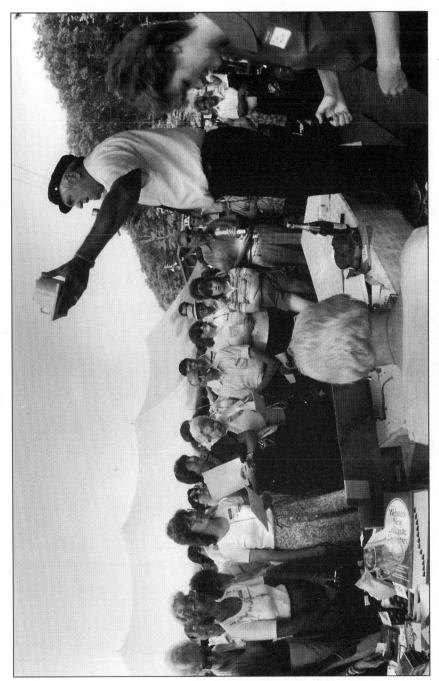

Silvio conducting auction at Mt. Tom, MA picnic, 1982. *Vincent D'Addario Photograph*

Silvio and his pal, Carl Yazstremski, fishing in Alaska, 1984. *Conte Family Photograph*

Congressman Conte with Polish President Lech Walesa, late 1980s.
Conte Family Photograph

Silvio wearing a pig mask to protest pork barrel spending, 1985.
Kenneth Garrett Photograph

Silvio in his tomato garden Bethesda, MD, 1985. *Kenneth Garrett Photograph*

Silvio at the dedication of the Boston University Medical Research Center, 1985.
Vincent D'Addario Photograph

Congressman Conte at his desk in 2300 Rayburn House Office Building, 1985.
Kenneth Garrett Photograph

Silvio O'Conte marching in the 1985 Holyoke St. Patrick's Day parade with grandsons Ryan and Jason Webb.
Vincent D'Addario Photograph

PORK BARREL FIGHTER

"If the only way to defeat that bill is with ridicule,
I'll try to ridicule it to death.
—*Silvio O. Conte, 1975*

Silvio Conte thought himself a great battler of "pork barrel" projects and was a consistent opponent of agricultural subsidies, big water projects and some jobs and public works programs. Because of his position on the Appropriations Committee he was called by some, "The King of Pork," for all of the funding he personally sponsored. Yet his battles to curb some aspects of government spending were remarkably consistent through the years and, most always, were fought with humor to cast the questioned funding in a bad light.

Some of Silvio's assaults were directed at waste in the Congress. In his first year, 1959, he fought the Congressional Franking Privilege for what he called "junk mail." He noted that much of it was returned and was accumulating in the Capitol basement, creating a fire hazard, "a camel caravan of a million pieces."

In 1963, Silvio encountered the wrath of Massachusetts Democrats for voting against a public works bill—Area Redevelopment Administration (ARA)—which gave local assistance grants. Silvio firmly stood his ground, explaining that both measures were wasteful boondoggles which would actually hurt New England. The ARA would fund the relocation of a shoe factory from Massachusetts to the midwest, grants to southern motels which still practiced segregation, construction of a new hotel in Detroit which had only a 54% occupancy rate, airport expansion for a town of 2,800 in Nevada, etc.

In 1971, after the third stereo was stolen from his car while parked in the Capitol garage Silvio went on a 20 year rampage against the Capitol police. "I think that if the 86-member police force of my home city of Pittsfield were substituted for the Capitol force of Keystones we would be much more secure in the Capitol area and the savings would be astronomic." The failure to protect those stereos along with other abuses—largely excessive spending requests—continued to fuel Silvio's ire. Eighteen years later in 1989 he took another shot at their funding request on the House floor.

"My target could regrettably be described Fortress Capitol. My target is the alarming growth of the number and equipment of the United States Capitol Police. Since Fiscal Year 1982 the number of Capitol Police positions has grown by 177 positions to a grand total of, listen to this, 1340, one-thousand three-hundred and forty people guard nine buildings and the surrounding grounds and they ask for 78 more positions in this budget, and thank God, we didn't give it to them. It costs $1,178,000 to dress up and equip each and every one of these officers. That cost alone has gone up 25% since 1982. It takes up a full single-spaced page just to list all the equipment we're buying for each officer. It's a wonder they can even walk with all the equipment they've got. I'm worried they're going to get hernias. Not that they have to walk anyway, since 1982 the Capitol Police fleet has gone from 70 to 132, an increase of 90%. They have, listen to this, a Ram Charger, a Cushman, three Surburbans, two buses, four Blazers, four trucks, five station wagons, five special vehicles, eleven vans, forty-five sedans and, get this, fifty motorcycles. They make the Shriners look like pikers. I just thought of that one. When you have all those bodies and all that equipment you've got to have a bureaucracy. Their organization chart looks like the Pentagon. The department now has bureaus, divisions, sections, units, teams, officers—even a special events section if you get caught in a telephone booth and can't figure out how to get out. I know this sounds like a joke, but it isn't. It's expensive. Mr. Chairman, Members of the House, this is enough. Someone is building an empire right over here under our noses. We have all these bodies stumbling over each other, we have police vehicles up to here. It's terrible, it's frightening to go anywhere and still they ask for more. In the name of security they've given us a monster. It's time to get this situation under control. We run this place, not the officers. I worry every morning when I drive in here. You go into the garage. There are four garage attendants and three policemen to back them up. I'm afraid I'm going to run over them. When are we going to stop this folly?"

Silvio frequently had trouble with Jobs Bills. He viewed many as big pork barrel packages. In 1975 he gave halfhearted support to one, say-ing, "I support the commitment of $1.625 billion to the Public Services of Jobs Program. At best this is an exercise in blowing up a leaky balloon. It's not sufficient just to create jobs for the sake of creating jobs. The Congress must start demanding a permanent return on its investment." Silvio's inter-est in legislation was always focused on its substance. What are the details? Where will the money go and what will we get for it? These were the ques-tions Silvio researched as he decided what to support, not support or most likely amend.

In 1977 he filed an amendment to repeal the Beekeepers Indemnity Program, started in 1970 to compensate beekeepers for destruction caused by government application of pesticides. In his "To bee or not to bee" speech Silvio pointed out that this program had long fulfilled its intended purpose and should be eliminated because he was "buzzing with waspish dismay." The bee program provided Silvio with some of his best theater for the next 15 years. Every year he had a new angle to eliminate this subsidy.

One year on the floor he said, "There is an old Scottish song 'I got a Bee in Ma Bonnet and Ma Honey on Ma Mind.' Too many beekeepers are running around singing 'I got Dead Bees in Ma Bonnet and Federal Money on Ma Mind.' During another year's debate he introduced an amendment to kill the honey subsidy and asked, "Do we go out and pay a guy in North Dakota $1 million for support prices for bees? Is that conscionable I ask? Or $257 million in support prices for four years. Is that conscionable? We're having trouble with the imports of shoes. Why don't we amend this bill and set up warehouses and store millions and billions of pairs of shoes? We've got another problem up there with panty hose. We're getting an in-flux of panty hose from Korea and Hong Kong. How about amending this bill to set up warehouses and we'll store millions and millions of dozens of panty hose? Before this program they had another bee program which I finally killed. It took me about 10 years to kill it. They were paying beekeep-ers for dead bees. They never had one autopsy on any of these bees to see if they died of a heart attack, arthritis or makin' love. They were paying these same beekeepers millions and millions of dollars because of dead bees and I finally killed the program and then they came around with this program which is worse than the other program. This is ridiculous."

He received nationwide coverage for fighting some small specific appropriations in 1990. The first was a line item in the Agricultural Appropriation of which he said "The conference report plays a different tune. If you listen closely, you can hear the sounds of champagne music wafting over from the Senate. You know what that is? It is Lawrence Welk pumping that accordion because this bill contains a $500,000 earmark to restore his birthplace in North Dakota . . . what will they do for an encore? Earmark funds to renovate Guy Lombardo's speed boat or restore Artie Shaw's tuxedo? There's more Mr. Speaker. There is also a $1 million earmark in the same account for the Institute of Decision Making in Iowa . . . It would have been appropriate to locate the Institute here in Washington. It's too bad this institute was not set up before the Senate decided to spend $500,000 on Lawrence Welk."

Another target which he attacked was SETI, the Search for Extra Terrestrial Intelligence, a program which he finally killed after some years of struggle in part due to an entertaining floor speech.

"Mr. Chairman, at a time when good people of America can't find affordable housing, we shouldn't be spending precious dollars to look for little green men with misshapen heads. It's time to put this crippled dog out of its misery and kill it with a forceful blow. Mr. Chairman, of course there are space aliens and advanced civilizations in outer space. But we don't need to spend $6 million this year to find evidence of these rascally creatures. We only need 75 cents to buy a tabloid at the local supermarket. Conclusive evidence of these crafty critters can be found at the checkout counters from coast to coast. This article, Exhibit 1, from the Weekly World News, for example, describes how UFO's were poised to land at Chicago's Soldier Field during halftime of last year's Bears-Eagles game. They were scared off, though, by gridlock traffic of blimps, helicopters and airplanes over the stadium. We also know that Noah's Ark was built by space aliens. I submit Exhibit 2 that I have here in my file. Why spend $5 million to search for radio waves, when we already know that space aliens are stealing our frogs. I submit for the record Exhibit 3. This intergalactic frog and tadpole theft, reported by hundreds of eyewitnesses, has become a serious global problem. Perhaps $6 million could be better spent by the Attorney General in bringing these orbiting scofflaws to justice. We know that a UFO blasted out of the ocean and hovered 16 terrifying minutes over a frightened Sri Lankan tanker crew, and we also know that this UFO cured 22 sick, blind and lame people in Turkey. This amendment gives us a chance to prove that there is still intelligent life on earth. Let us save our hard-earned money and let the space aliens spend their currency to find us. We should seriously consider the funding of an even more ambitious program, SCI: Search for Congressional Intelligence."

Many of Silvio's assaults against funding projects never made it out of committee. He killed or reduced many agricultural and defense proposals before they got on the House floor. But those battles which C-SPAN covered on the floor provided the nation with much entertainment.

ENVIRONMENTALIST

"Always remember that we have an obligation to
pass on the natural environment of the world to the
next generation intact or improved. Love, Nonno."
—*Silvio O. Conte, 1990*
(Inscription to his grand-children in a book about
Antarctica)

 S ilvio Conte was an environmentalist before there were environmentalists. As a teenager during the Great Depression he would enjoy the outdoors, pick berries and catch frogs when he walked along Dalton Division Road to work on a farm. From this time until the end of his life he was in awe of nature's beauty and, once he entered public office, constantly worked to protect the environment. In the State Senate he supported water pollution and conservation legislation as well as park improvements for the Berkshires.

In the Congress Silvio quickly became a national environmental champion. In his first year, 1959, he sided with Senator John F. Kennedy and his other Massachusetts colleagues on a bill to create the Cape Cod National Seashore Park. Explaining his stand, Silvio said about the Cape that "the future will be the loser and a national resource will go the way of amusement parks, pizza palaces, hot dog stands and miles of cottages that destroy the beauty that their owners come to enjoy." The following year Silvio voted to override President Eisenhower's veto of a water pollution control bill. In 1962 he authored and got passed legislation to protect the bald eagle. In 1969 he authored a bill making the wolf, coyote, mountain lion, bobcat and bear endangered species.

Silvio's love of hunting, fishing and the outdoors strongly affected his legislative views. His admiration for Theodore Roosevelt was largely based upon his efforts to preserve wildlife habitats. In 1967, as a member of the Migratory Bird Commission, he went to St. Vincent's Island in Florida to inspect this area as a possible wildlife refuge. This was the beginning of a long series of visits and subsequent refuge designations in which Silvio participated throughout his Congressional years. The Sierra Club, National Audubon Society, Wilderness Society, and others gave him a Conservation Certificate which said, "Silvio Conte is no armchair conservationist. He moves. He not only files legislation for conservation but fights for it. His interests are not restricted to his own district but to natural resources in all sections. He was only one of four members of Congress who were able to prevail on a majority of their colleagues to hold up passage of a bill which would have created two dams in the Grand Canyon."

In 1965 the Dickey-Lincoln hydroelectric project in Northern Maine was authorized by the Congress. Silvio protested because no environmental or detailed economic study had been made. The project had the support of many New England members because of high electric rates in the region. Any plans to increase electrical output were favorably received, especially after the November 1965 blackout. This project would have constructed a dam on the St. John River that would have flooded some 89,000 wooded acres. The lake created would fill during spring floods and snow melts and then be let through the spillway during the daytime to generate power. The water would then be held and pumped back up above the dam at night to generate more power the next day. A Congressional delegation, including Silvio and Congressman Tip O'Neill, journeyed to the proposed site in northwestern Maine, the Allagash Wilderness, a remote area with no roads or towns nearby. Enthusiasm was dampened when, during the presentation of the project's virtues, Silvio hollered, "Stop, stop. This is the last wilderness and this project is a disaster. Birds will die and fish will have no place to live. We just cannot do this." Everyone was dismayed when Silvio promised that when he returned to Washington he would do everything he could to stop it, particularly by seeing that it received no appropriations. Once back in Washington, Silvio and his staff began to do their own research, and with the assistance of GAO they demonstrated that promised benefits were overstated. Environmentalists rallied to work with Silvio with the battle cry, "Are we going to destroy the Maine wilderness to run air conditioners in Boston?" Also emphasized was the bathtub ring effect which would result as water levels on the shoreline fluctuated by as much as 75 feet. Silvio used his legislative skills and wiles to curtail funding for years. Delay along with the eventual determination that the project was of dubious benefit killed Dickey-Lincoln. For Silvio this struggle was not without political cost, and he later said, "That project was an environmental outrage but my colleagues made me feel like a skunk at a lawn party for opposing it. I was accused of trying to ruin the New England economy. Some of my good friends in the delegation would walk the other way when they saw me coming."

The tenacity that was a hallmark of Silvio's entire Congressional service was illustrated by work with Dickey-Lincoln. In 1974, the 10th year that this came up for funding, saw, despite Silvio's objections, $800,000 appropriated for planning. The energy crisis sparked new interest in this project, especially among New England members. For a short time it appeared that Silvio would be the sole New Englander to vote no. His friend Bob Giaimo, convinced that the project was uneconomic, finally joined Silvio along with two other New Englanders. After the vote, Silvio vowed to continue to fight, still believing the project an environmental disaster. He said that despite the planning funds the project was still a long way from being started. He explained his position in an interview in a magazine, *MASSACHUSETTS WILDLIFE*, in late 1974. In response to the question, "Don't you think you're putting your head in the chopping block by bucking everyone on this," he replied, "Maybe for the short term, but I don't care. I know I'm right. In Maine they say who are you from Massachusetts coming up here and telling us what to do with our river? What these people don't realize is it's not just their river; it belongs to the whole country. It's yours and it's mine, and once it's gone, it's gone forever. There's no way of getting it back. That's why it's so important to stick your nose in there and fight."

Silvio pointed out in an interview the same year, "I think I've survived because I stick with an issue, and a lot of times I've been proved right." These sometimes unpopular stands were backed by careful and painstaking staff work which always provided Silvio with solid factual material to support his position. Dickey-Lincoln was a major issue in the 1974 Congressional race when Silvio was challenged by a Pittsfield attorney who questioned Silvio's opposition to lower power rates. This caused no change in his stand.

By 1977 the Dickey-Lincoln dam was still being funded for planning, but starting to wane. Silvio offered a substitute bill with $123 million to modernize other New England hydroelectric plants to replace the power from Dickey-Lincoln, which would have cost $1 billion to build. President Carter placed Dickey-Lincoln on a list for elimination and the environmentalists helped by pointing out that the furbish lousewort (a wild snapdragon) habitat was endangered by the proposed flooding. Finally, in 1979 Dickey-Lincoln was killed for good.

From his early years in the Congress Silvio assumed responsibility for looking out for the environment. He was particularly wary of large water projects. In his view they not only were damaging to land and wildlife but they were overly expensive compared to their benefits. He fought many projects, including the Tennessee-Tombigbee project, much of which was in the district of Appropriations Chairman Jamie Whitten of Mississippi. Chairman Whitten sometimes said that Silvio's anti-pork barrel speeches were a smokescreen to cover his own pork projects, but Silvio's efforts were based on the long held conviction that habitats should be preserved. "I can go to a stream and just sit there and watch when the dew is up and watch a rabbit come prancing by. These are great things, great treasures." He was not a freshly minted environmentalist. He felt the same way in the 1930s and 1940s and 1950s. In the Congress he could get a good audience for his outrage and he had the staff resources to investigate the precise effects of many projects. One he particularly did not like was the "Oregon Inlet Jetties," a Corps of Engineers proposal to construct jetties near the Cape Hatteras, North Carolina National Seashore. Silvio was outraged by the project effects, its cost and by being told he should leave it alone because it was not in his district. "Mr. Chairman, it's not often that we can stop a bad project before it's underway. Scientific opinion is unanimous on the damage to the Federally protected seashore and wildlife refuge in this area. And taxpayers' opinion should be unanimous that this is a useless way to waste $100 million. Let's kill it now. My good friend from New Jersey, Mr. Roe, has chastised us that we don't live in the district and therefore we should pass everything any Congressman brings in here whether it's good or bad, because he's from the district. Well, let me tell you something, I was elected by half a million people in my Congressional District and it's the taxpayers' money—not Mr. Roe's money—it's the taxpayers' money. I've got a right to stand up here and fight against a $100 million boondoggle in North Carolina, New Jersey, California or any other place. I paid $45,000 in Federal taxes last year. It's my money and I don't want my money going down there for this boondoggle."

In the same way that the late 1960s and 1970s were consumed fighting Dickey-Lincoln, the Garrison Diversion Project in North Dakota took over in the 1980s. Silvio was appalled by this huge project more than a thousand miles from home. It would realign watercourses, dry up old waterways and destroy wildlife habitats. Silvio fought this for years and received a good deal of media coverage for his efforts both on and off the House floor. "Let me go on with this disaster. They would require the construction of the first phase under this Senate amendment of three of this environmentally ruinous maze of canals, dams and reservoirs which have skyrocketed from $207 million—HO HO—get this: to $1 billion, $1 billion, I said $1 billion dollars. The other gentleman from Alabama says, why nobody objecting lives within 200 miles of this project. There are many taxpayers paying for this boondoggle. I don't care if it's 5,000 miles away, my taxpayers are paying for this and I've got a right to oppose this. Who are we, a bunch of tin gods up here?"

One day Silvio brought a pig mask to the floor, black glasses with a plastic hog snout attached. He wanted to wear it on the floor to protest all the members "slopping up all the pork in the trough" but Speaker O'Neill told him that the Sergeant-at-Arms would remove him from the Floor for insulting the dignity of the House, so Silvio retreated to a press conference which made all the network news programs all over the country. *The Greenfield Record* described him in action saying, "He sometimes appears to be conducting a hyperactive orchestra as he stands at the podium frantically swinging his arms and screaming almost loud enough to rattle the dishes in the House restaurant on the floor below." A North Dakota newspaper called him "the Massachusetts Mouth." Yet his persistence worked, and moderate changes to scale back the project were eventually achieved. Silvio summed it up: "If North Dakota is entitled to a water project and I'm not saying that they're not, let's sit down like sane people and let's try to negotiate and compromise this thing. Give them some water without costing a billion-two, without destroying the environment and without destroying our relationship with our neighbors to the north."

In much the same way that Silvio fought the Garrison Diversion Project, he battled for legislation to curb acid rain. He waged this struggle alone for an extended period of time during which no one in the Congress except himself believed that there was any chance of success. Silvio's concern came directly from the eastern part of his district when he learned in 1983 that Quabbin Reservoir could not be stocked with trout because the water's acidity was too great. Silvio set up a task force to investigate the causes of this problem. From this he learned that sulphur dioxide emissions from smokestacks in the midwest were being carried eastward by the prevailing winds and being deposited in the northeastern United States and eastern Canada. Silvio's contentions were subjected to ridicule by the Reagan administration and strong opposition from the Energy and Commerce Committee, responsible for regulatory legislation to deal with such a problem. In 1984 Silvio described the effect of the "Acid Rain of Terror" from his study which found some 70 bodies of water in New England were acidified or "dead." In 1985 Silvio introduced legislation to require a tax on utility customers to pay for the cost of reducing sulphur dioxide emissions. This was killed by the Energy and Commerce Committee, dominated by members from the midwest which was heavily dependent upon high sulphur coal for industrial and commercial power generation. Similar legislation was introduced and defeated again and again. Silvio criticized President Reagan and the EPA for inaction on this problem in 1987. It was not until 1989 when his old friend President Bush was in the White House that Silvio got a commitment from the President to give it attention. Finally the Clean Air Act of 1990 was passed with a provision for mandated reductions in sulphur dioxide emissions. Silvio proudly stood by as the President signed this legislation.

For 26 years Silvio served on the Migratory Bird Commission, an adjunct of the Department of Interior's Fish and Wildlife Service. This Commission met to decide on the disposition of the proceeds for the sale of the annual duck stamp to hunters. These funds, which averaged between $20 and $25 million each year, were required by law to be used to purchase land for wildlife refuges. According to the service, "During Mr. Conte's tenure the Commission protected nearly three million acres of waterfowl habitat. Eighty new wildlife refuges totalling over one million acres were also approved while Mr. Conte was on the Commission."

Silvio's last wildlife project was one on which he worked right up until his death. This project involved the entire Connecticut River and its approach was completely new. All previous refuge projects had specific tracts of land set aside to protect one or more species. The Connecticut River

Wildlife Refuge, spanning the four states, was designated to protect fish, bird and plant populations, protect and enhance the ecosystems, identify endangered species and provide for research and recreation. This project was comprehensive and sought to study the entire river system by coordinating state and local data and planning functions to determine new ways to protect the river—easements, land purchases, donations of land, etc. This legislation, creating the Silvio O. Conte National Fish and Wildlife Refuge, was passed by Congress in 1991, the year of Silvio's death, and signed into law by President Bush in December of that year. An important reason for the passage of this legislation was the intense work, including testifying before committees, that Corinne did in 1991 to honor Silvio, who cared so much for preserving and improving the Connecticut River.

COOK

"C'mon over for dinner."
—*Silvio O. Conte*

*F*ood played an important part in Silvio's life and Congressional career. He inherited the love for good food and good cooking from his mother. He continued her tradition of serving good food to many gathered around the kitchen table, starting in Pittsfield where, as a State Senator, he frequently invited people to his mother's home.

In Washington his table became a well known gathering place. Corinne often had no idea how many people were coming to dinner until they all showed up—trying as a general rule to keep enough food on hand for 15 more people than she expected. Silvio often made polenta or soup to feed extra mouths. His specialties were many—roast pheasant, quail, roasts, stews, soups often using his own game. Every August he went salmon fishing in Alaska and brought back his catch to be served at his Labor Day party and his Washington birthday party at the Botanic Garden. These events signified his inclusive spirit. He wanted to have everyone he ever met over for dinner. The preparation of his salmon was done by Silvio with surgical precision. He sat at his kitchen table at Onota Lake in Pittsfield with his $3.95 half-glasses perched on the end of his nose filleting and thinly slicing the salmon to make lox. Any stray bones were carefully removed with tweezers as he puffed on a large cigar. Only occasionally were his children allowed to help, maybe chopping onions if done just right.

Sometimes he held dinners for the State Department whose officials would ask him to entertain and feed a particularly difficult delegation. Silvio would fill them with barbecued steaks, roasts or pasta as well as vodka and wine, leaving any group much more congenial then when it had arrived. He started a Columbus Day lunch for his Italian-American colleagues, but it soon became popular with other members because of Fran McGuire's escarole soup and lasagna and Silvio's good cheer which he provided wearing a white apron and chef's hat.

One day Corinne decided to make chili. She had just sold a house to a Texas family of whom she asked, "How do you flavor your chili? Ours always comes out like spaghetti sauce." "A can of jalapeno peppers finely chopped with all stems and seeds added." When Silvio tasted the new concoction which Flora, a family friend, and Corinne had just prepared, he said, "Let's enter this in the Congressional chili contest as Chili con Conte." Silvio added some wine and rosemary, basil and thyme and took it to the House. Later he came home with a large award for winning first prize. Soon he was getting requests for the recipe, asking Corinne, "How did you make that stuff?

His weekends at home involved preparing meals for whatever friends and family he encountered on his whirlwind First District journeys. Often he would go to his favorite eating place—his sister Betty's kitchen in Pittsfield. Betty was heir to their mother's recipes and would spend hours preparing Silvio's favorite dishes, those he remembered from his mother's kitchen. If he thought he would like one of these specialties that was not too time consuming to prepare, he would call Betty himself and say he was coming. If he wanted one of his more difficult favorites such as risotto with chicken livers or roast pheasant, he would have his Pittsfield office call Betty and make the request. Betty would tell Silvio that it was too much work but she would not turn down an official office request.

Occasionally Betty was called upon to entertain his guests. Early one week Silvio convinced Betty to make polenta baccala, a very time-consuming procedure because the dried fish had to be carefully soaked for a day and then the sauce and polenta had to be prepared. In the beginning of the week Silvio announced he would be in on Friday and would have a guest. The next day it was two guests and the day after it was three. On Friday morning Silvio stopped by to make sure everything was in order. Betty was concerned that maybe the guests would not like this unusual Italian dish. Silvio said, "Don't worry, everybody always loves whatever you make." As he walked through the house he noticed the dining room table was set with Betty's good china and linens and asked "Who the hell is coming to dinner?" Betty replied that it was for his guests. Silvio said, "Put all of this away. We have to eat in the kitchen. The dining room is no place for polenta baccala." The dinner was a great success and everyone had multiple servings.

To Silvio, Washington was a backward place when it came to food. Except for excursions to his favorite Alpine Restaurant in Arlington, run by his friends, Ermanno and Pino, who would prepare polenta to go with fish, quail and other game he brought in to be cooked, Silvio usually ate at home. For these meals he would bring fresh foods as well as plants from his garden back to Washington.

Nan, his Pittsfield officer manager, always knew that if he left before the last minute for Bradley Airport that there would be a few stops. "First we have to stop at Betty and Joe's house to pick up some rosemary plants for the garden." Then to Pittsfield Rye Bakers to get two large loaves of bread, one carried under each arm onto the plane, and a bag of rolls. Then to Springfield "we're having some people over and I have to get some cheese." Nan would say, "You look like an old farmer—not an important Congressman—with all those plastic and paper bags." "I gotta do this because you can't get good stuff in Washington." What Silvio could get in Washington was fresh tomatoes picked from the hundreds of tomato plants in this backyard, along with zucchini, garlic, rosemary and basil, with the entire garden bordered by Dirksen marigolds.

In early spring Silvio started his tomato plants from seeds and every window in his house was filled with boxes of sprouts. A few plants would not do. He had to have hundreds in order to give away large bags of tomatoes every day to his many friends on the Hill. This was the only agriculture program that Silvio thought was any good—it fed lots of people and its cost was low.

This was very much a family affair. Corinne watered the seedlings every day. Silvio's youngest daughter, Gayle, would come and prepare the garden and then plant the seedlings outside once the weather permitted. Gayle frequently took care of Silvio when Corinne returned to Pittsfield during the summer and had the opportunity to do much of Silvio's garden work, too.

EDUCATOR

"Education is the key to opening doors that have
been closed by opposition, ignorance and injustice."
—*Silvio O. Conte*
(Dedication of Conte Forum Boston College, 1989)

T he focus of Silvio's greatest effort and attention throughout his entire career was education. He said over and over that his education at Boston College made his career possible. While George Bush was President, Silvio would occasionally go to the White House to have a drink with President and Mrs. Bush. Once home he would always tell Corinne how much he appreciated his education. "How else would a poor Italian boy like me ever get to go to the White House?" Silvio's greatest dream for the country was to make the opportunity which he had for college education available to every American. He often said, "The ability to attend college should not be denied for financial reasons."

In the area of education, Silvio was not noted for authoring or having passed any single bill. His work in education highlights his often stated desire to be known as "a work horse, not a show horse." From his early days in the Massachusetts State Senate until his death he worked diligently every year to improve educational opportunities for Americans. In the Senate he supported expansion of the University of Massachusetts (UMASS) at Amherst. Although not in his senatorial district, it would serve many of his constituents.

Once in Congress, Silvio worked every year to get more resources allocated to education. He took pride in the fact that Federal funding for education increased from $1.4 billion in 1958 to $26 billion in 1990. In 1962 Silvio introduced legislation to provide Federal funds for college classroom construction and scholarships. The following year he introduced a bill to provide families with a tax deduction of $1,000 for college expenses and another bill to provide $1.5 billion in federal funds for educational purposes. In 1965 he filed a bill to provide educational "GI" benefits for those who were serving in "whatever we call what is going on in Vietnam." In 1971 Silvio obtained a seat on the Labor-Health-Education Appropriations Subcommittee. This gave him much more input on funding for education projects and helped him secure many grants each year for colleges and universities both in and out of his district. Silvio was proud of any funds he could direct toward education and never relented in their pursuit. As he rose in seniority on this subcommittee, Silvio assigned himself the task of looking out for the student loan programs and Pell grants. He always cited his good fortune in having the GI Bill get him through Boston College. Securing educational grants and scholarships was a task Silvio performed day in and day out for years. He watched over this all the time.

He also fought for funding for elementary and secondary education, for vocational programs and for assistance for the disabled and disadvantaged. He augmented this effort whenever he could by getting funds for libraries and specific college programs such as drives to improve foreign language teaching at colleges and universities. For this effort, Silvio received many honorary degrees and the chance to make commencement speeches. Staffers said that Silvio gave as much attention to preparation of a high school or college speech as he did to a meeting with the President.

In 1988, an experience in his own district realigned national education policy. Sandy Thomas of Greenfield, the mother of a child with Attention Deficit Disorder (A.D.D.), sought to learn about this condition for which there was little information, help or support. After months of research, she called Silvio's Pittsfield office to see if there was anything at the Federal level for this. Shortly she received some information from the office and also a call from Pittsfield that Silvio would be coming to a veterans affair in Greenfield soon and would like to meet her. A few days later Sandy received a telephone call from a man with a loud voice who said, "This is Sil Conte. I want to talk with you about A.D.D. and need more time so please meet me at the police station at 11 o'clock."

At the appointed time he drove up in "his old red car" all by himself. "The two of us sat on a bench outside and talked about this for an hour and half. He listened with fascination as I explained that this is not a matter of children not trying hard enough. They just cannot understand and nowhere is this recognized as a problem." Silvio replied that he was very interested in this and wanted her to come to Washington to see some people. Silvio also told her that he had a feeling that perhaps as a child he had some of this problem because he had great difficulty with some school subjects.

When Sandy got to Washington she was sent to see some of the top people at the Department of Education. After three years and 30 trips to Washington to testify before Congress and the Department of Education, she saw A.D.D. recognized by Federal law with funding which provided for study and A.D.D. centers. These were established solely because of Silvio's interest and follow through. Sandy relates that on many Washington trips Silvio personally spoke with her, encouraged her and counseled her. She said, "Because of his dedication he empowered parents to work with the schools to help these children. For those of us that worked with him on this he made us feel like members of the family. He inspired us to reach down and pull the best out of ourselves. He really represented the people."

STYLE

> "At 52 he exudes an almost boyish enthusiasm
> whether detailing the merits of a piece of
> legislation or telling a joke."
> —*Boston Globe, 1974*

*B*eyond the skill and knowledge Silvio brought to the Capitol, he offered an unequalled style. No matter what happened he maintained his magnificent humor. "I never try to take myself too seriously. There are a lot of big egos in this town and sometimes you just have to laugh at it all." He ended a serious commencement speech in Holyoke by saying, "In closing, let me call upon one of my great Italian ancestors who said 'Svegliati amico, discorso e finito' which means wake up, pal, the speech is over."

On the House floor his excitement sometimes made him become increasingly irate, causing one colleague to remark that Silvio was "the only man who is infuriated by the sound of his own voice." Colleagues frequently declared, "There was no one like Silvio." He took many tough, controversial positions but was able to diffuse animosity with humor. Also as longtime friend and colleague, Dante Fascell, said, "he was always graceful." He had a great sense of drama. Once at the most suspenseful time facing the Appropriations Committee, the time when the entire Federal budget is allocated to the 13 subcommittees so they can begin their work, Silvio announced the amounts just like the Academy awards. "This year's winner is Labor, Health and Human Service with . . . Billion, second is Defense with . . . Billion", handing each chairman a small statue as the amount was declared. Appropriations Chairman Jamie Whitten said, "Silvio was a rhymester, not a poet." Yet he used often hilarious verse to make a point, diffuse tension and move the process along.

In one Medicare debate he gave another member the "Italian Salute" to protest the failure to bring an amendment to a vote. Everyone was greatly amused by this except his sister, Betty, who called to tell him it was undignified and demeaning to their Italian heritage. Once he was chastised by one of the Republican House leaders for going along with the Democrats on raising the debt ceiling to keep the government running. Silvio replied that some day the Republicans would be in charge and would need this. A few years later this was the case and the Republican President needed the same vote. At a party luncheon Silvio put a large veiled object in front of this leader and said, "Here's your lunch." It was a model of a large crow from the Smithsonian.

One day at a Foreign Aid hearing, Silvio read the newspaper while other members argued bitterly about which country should get what. After finishing the paper, Silvio reached into his briefcase, pulled out some darts and flung them at the world map on the wall saying, "Why don't we just allocate the money like that. It makes more sense than what we're doing here today." Frustrated by the delays Congress was encountering getting its work done because of extended emotional debates on highly controversial issues which were never resolved, Silvio proposed "Gladiator Week." The Congress would take one week and "fight to the death" about emotionally charged issues such as school prayer, abortion, legal aid, leaving the rest of the year to do regular work.

The advent of cable television gave Silvio a new forum, C-SPAN. He did not appear on network talk shows but did C-SPAN interviews and appeared most every day the House was in session on the live House TV coverage. In 1983 he was interviewed on the first C-SPAN interview before a live audience asking questions. This came in the midst of the debate over the "Jobs Bill" and the Social Security reform.

Of the Jobs Bill he said "This is the third time I fought this jobs bill, I think just the fact that they place this label 'jobs bill' on it with the high unemployment we have in this country is really tragic. They think you can get anything through. I am very disturbed about the jobs bill. It was a $4.6 billion package. It was hastily put together. There were things in there I never heard of. They had $50 million for SBA to plant trees. Can you imagine me going back to my small businessman in Western Massachusetts who's in trouble and in dire need of every dollar he can get and then saying I put $50 million in this bill to plant trees. Thirty-two million dollars in there for a demonstration road in Mississippi. Where's it going to be? We checked it out. What's so hot about this demonstration road. My chairman ain't going to be too happy with me. It's in his district. It's a two-lane highway and they're going to make it a four-lane highway. Now isn't that great. The thing was filled with pet projects for certain Congressmen. This wan't the kind of jobs bill I was looking for. I was looking for one that was highly labor intensive with lasting benefit—improve rail beds, water systems, forestry work, CCC camps. You know I said it was like taking a pig in a butcher shop and getting the Cardinals (Appropriations Subcommittee Chairmen) up there - the Kingpins and kill the hog and cut the hog up and divide it and take off out the back door with their prize piece of hog and then they open the front door and let the rest of the Congress in and this is what they get, (as he pulled a rubber chicken out of his briefcase). That's what the job bill does." Rubber chickens had to appear in interviews or news conferences because they were prohibited on the House floor.

Live television coverage of the House proceedings allowed Silvio's style to be seen nationwide. His silver gray hair, his half-glasses on the end of his nose, his arms waving, his brightly colored jackets and ties, his clashing plaids and stripes, his entire bearing gave the House an electric aura when Silvio went to the well to speak. Members and staff often said that he was the only one who made them actually stop and listen. He was excited, exciting, passionate, funny, enthusiastic and totally absorbed with whatever he was discussing. Silvio added life and passion to a process which had become dreary. In an era of pollsters, consultants and hair stylists, Silvio limped to the podium, said his piece, slapped his papers down on the clerk's desk and walked up the aisle. After one of his famous outbursts of temper, he would laugh by the time he was three rows up the aisle, either putting his arm around the member whom he had just denounced or winking at another member saying, "How did you like that?"

On some occasions Silvio influenced specific legislation with his floor speeches, tirades and jokes, but most of his legislative "heavy lifting" was done in Committee with hard work and perserverence along with exhaustive and excellent staff work, but he added humor and life and moved the process along. He said many times, "Nobody in this place knows how to have a good time anymore."

Silvio was a man of many contrasts, contrasts which defined him much more than labels or ideology because he could balance and blend opposing ideas, views and beliefs. He was fiercely proud of his Italian heritage and a sentimental American patriot. He was a hard nosed practical politician who could mobilize every crafty strategy known in Washington, yet he had a strong faith in the open process and often stated his opinion that everyone should have a voice. Some said he was an egotistical publicity hound, yet he stayed off the television talk shows, only occasionally doing C-SPAN or local interviews to give a detailed explanation of a particular issue or set of issues. He said, "I do my bit here."

He was staunchly anti-abortion, but a strong supporter of planned parenthood. He was branded by one conservative group as a tax and spend liberal who "almost never votes right" yet the National Taxpayers Union said, "He's certainly been helpful in going after the big pork barrel projects." He worked hard and played hard, too. No one was more serious or intense about the nation's real issues and no one in the Capitol could be more slapstick or ridiculous. He could be impossible at one moment, especially with family or staff, and then look to them for a laugh or a good time. He was bold and forward looking such as when he proposed Acid Rain curbs, AIDS funding, etc., yet took on no cause without carefully reviewing the facts to assure that he stood on firm ground. He was renowned for his ability to fashion political accords and excelled at piecing together agreements from many disparate and conflicting factions but he could also be confrontational in the same process. "Would it be out of order to call him a cheap, irresponsible demagogue?"

He maintained a frenetic and at times frantic schedule, sometimes physically impossible to keep, yet when talking to his constituents he gave the impression that he had all day to listen to what they had to say. Silvio knew all the subtleties and nuances of the trade yet he was exceedingly direct and incisive. At a Congressional hearing debating sharp curtailment of student loans, he asked Education Secretary Bell, "Can you honestly say that you think what you propose is a good idea?"

To constituents he was almost always extremely sympathetic, yet if one was trying to take advantage, Silvio would respond appropriately. One constituent came to the Pittsfield office looking for a Social Security disability because of alleged knee injuries which Silvio knew were not legitimate. When the pleader came into Silvio's office on crutches, Silvio pulled his pant legs above his knees saying, "You wanna see bad knees. I'll show you bad knees. Why don't you get the hell out of here and get rid of those crutches before you hurt yourself."

He could be tough and, at times, insensitive, yet tender and caring, especially for those in need. One evening he was dining with friends at his favorite Virginia restaurant, the Alpine, with singing, Italian music and accordion playing. Silvio looked over to a nearby table and saw a sad little girl with two older men. He invited her to come to his table and sat her in his lap and had songs sung and played for her and she began to smile and have a good time. After dinner one of the men came over and said thank you, explaining that this was the first time they had been to the Alpine since her mother had died and that today was her birthday, the first one without her mother so she was very sad, but that Silvio's attention along with the singing had made her smile and given her a happy birthday. As Silvio's good friend, Jim Desmond said, "He just looked over and instinctively felt that this little girl was in need."

CHAMPION OF BIO-MEDICAL RESEARCH

"The funding for cystic fibrosis will continue."
—*Silvio O. Conte, 1984*

Silvio maintained a keen interest in health care throughout his career. In the Massachusetts State Senate he was the author of a bill to provide health care for state and municipal employees. In 1965 and again in 1971, he called for comprehensive nationwide health care coverage. In 1971, he received assignment to the Labor-Health-Education Appropriations Subcommittee which funds federal health spending. From this position he sought funding for mental health through the Community Mental Health Centers Act, especially the provision which provided funding for building local centers. Both the Nixon and Ford Administrations would request zero funding, but Silvio managed to get $25 to $35 million appropriated each year through his position on the HHS Subcommittee and got a new center to serve Western Massachusetts. Although located outside his District, in Springfield, this facility was positioned to help many of his constituents.

In the mid-1970s Silvio obtained planning and construction funding for the Geriatric Authority of Holyoke to remake an existing building into a geriatric rehabilitation facility. Silvio was able to bring several of his passions together in this project. He was long concerned for the wellbeing of senior citizens. He saw his job as an opportunity to look out for those in need, especially those in need of health care. This unique facility opened in 1977 and provided rehabilitation care for the elderly. He was also able to help Holyoke, always a source of strong support.

One of Silvio's greatest interests became bio-medical research. He was fascinated by the new treatments and techniques being developed each year. In an interview in 1989 he stated that the most interesting part of the entire Appropriations process for him was learning about the annual progress of research in medicine. Silvio's support for medical research had two strong bases. He fervently believed that, because of the cost, meaningful research could be done only by the Federal government. There were not adequate resources anywhere else. On the personal level, he was moved by the plight of the many people who journeyed to testify at hearings or saw him privately to discuss their problems with illness. These eloquent statements spurred him to increase funding for many programs.

Silvio's sympathy for research coupled with his reputation as one of the most progressive and forward looking members of Congress caused a doctor from National Institutes of Health to approach him in 1979 to tell of a disease in Western Africa killing thousands of people. This malady, not yet named AIDS, he said would kill 100,000 Americans by the end of the century. Silvio worked with Labor, HHS Subcommittee Chairman Bill Natcher of Kentucky to get the first funds appropriated to study AIDS. Five years later he described this event: "We brought AIDS funding up to about $211 million. It's an amazing thing about this. Five years ago on the Appropriations Committee I had been trying to get more money for the National Institutes of Health and all of a sudden we were talking with a doctor from NIH and he mentioned AIDS. At that time there were about half a dozen cases in the United States. I discussed it with him and I did a radio show with him. After the hearing I put $9 million in, which was the first money we ever put in for AIDS. I went home and told my wife, who was a nurse, there is a new disease and she had never heard of it. I said this thing could spread just like the plague because it can be spread through blood transfusions, there are so many ways you can pick it up."

He called for the designation of an AIDS Czar in 1985 and the government finally caught up with him in 1993. Each year he was a strong champion of AIDS funding. In a floor debate introducing the funding for Fiscal Year 1988 he said, "None of the priority items in this bill should surprise anyone, AIDS Research and Prevention $945.4 million, nearly a billion dollars to try to find a cure for this scourge. They say in 1991 more people will die of AIDS then died in the entire World War II. It's frightening." AIDS research was only one of many diseases against which he fought so consistently to try to help NIH find a cure.

Each year he heard the stories of people with specific health problems testify as the annual research funding was being considered. His views were shaped by what individuals both from his district and the nation told him. Learning their difficulties led him to protect and enhance the research programs at the National Institutes of Health. Susan Tolchin, a board member of the Cystic Fibrosis Foundation, tells of a time in the mid-1980s when the administration proposed to eliminate all NIH funding for cystic fibrosis. At a meeting in Silvio's office, two leading NIH geneticists explained in great detail that finding a cure for this disease was hopeless and that further spending was wasteful. Susan related being devastated as she heard this while Silvio sat quietly, not saying a word. She was sure that this program was doomed. Silvio listened as she said that elimination of the NIH program would not only hurt research but also kill the impetus to do anything about the disease nationwide. The signal would be sent that it was useless to try to find a cure.

After this, Susan said, "As a mother of a child with cystic fibrosis, I ask only one question. Who represents the mothers?" Without hesitation, Silvio looked at her and said, "Don't worry, I represent the mothers. The program will continue." The experts were disturbed and asked why the Congressman did not take the advice of the qualified people in the field. To this Silvio replied, "That's just what the generals and admirals say when they come up here. Listen to us, we're the experts, we know what's best. Well, we don't always listen to them because sometimes they're wrong. Cystic fibrosis funding will continue." The funding did continue and in a few years a gene defect which caused this disease was discovered.

On the home front, another disease, Neurofibromatosis (NF), came to his attention in 1983 from one of his constituents, Claudette Kiley of Granby. She called to ask him to support a bill to help with this disease which afflicts about one out of every 4,000 Americans, causing scoliosis, learning disabilities, optic nerve damage, disfigurement and bone deformity resulting from small tumors on nerve endings. Mrs. Kiley called Silvio to ask him to support the bill and he replied, "Hey, kid, I'm with ya." She explained that almost no one knows anything about this ailment. Silvio told her that legislation was not always needed. "There are other ways to get the same job done." At first Mrs. Kiley was puzzled, but Silvio wrote to the NIH asking for a report on the disease, its extent, research and prospects for cure. With this request from an influential member of Congress, NF began to be taken seriously and funding requests began to come to the Appropriations Committee. Mrs. Kiley testified before a hushed audience about how her children were afflicted, convincing Silvio to convene a working committee to study this disease. Through Silvio's efforts, funding increased from $100,000 to several million dollars within five years for NF genetic research.

For 20 years Silvio was the key player in obtaining federal funding for specific disease research: cancer, AIDS, diabetes, arthritis, heart disease, myasthenia gravis, Lyme disease. A large new initiative was undertaken in 1989—designation of the 1990s "Decade of the Brain." Silvio had a long fascination with neurological problems and the research that could help them. The motivation was that 50 million Americans were suffering from some disability, neurological injury or disease, drug or alcohol abuse and other mental illnesses. In economic terms the annual cost was estimated to be $300 billion. This initiative, which President Bush also signed into law in late 1989, was Silvio's personal pledge to accelerate Federal funding for the National Institute of Mental Health.

120

CAMPAIGNER

"The Conte record is almost invulnerable to
effective attack."
—*BERKSHIRE EAGLE, 1976*

*A*s a campaign team, Corinne and Silvio were without equal.
With family members and close friends they built an organization in
Pittsfield and expanded it throughout western Massachusetts. The Contes
and their people got out and saw the electorate from 1950 until 1990. They
maintained detailed notebooks, town by town, of contributors and volunteers. They had books indicating where to put up lawn signs, one of Silvio's
favorite campaign devices. He said that the lawn signs reminded people
enroute to polls for whom they should cast their ballot.

Silvio always ran on his own terms and would not bend to opponents' schedules or suggestions. As time passed he more and more ignored
his opponents, a tactic which infuriated the challenger. Results show that
this strategy worked. In 21 general elections, from 1950 to 1990, Silvio never
had a close election. In the first election for the Massachusetts State Senate,
Silvio received 55.4% of the vote while challenging a three term incumbent.
Silvio won in 1952 with 72.5% of the vote and with 73.9% in 1954. For his
fourth State Senate term in 1956, he received the nomination of both Republican and Democrats and ran unopposed. For his initial Congressional election in 1958, Silvio achieved 55.4% of the vote—a landslide to the papers—
a "squeaker" to him. This victory, the first of 17 for Congress, set the stage
for what was to become a rare, if not unique, political achievement.

By reelection time in 1960, Silvio's frequent trips home, along with
his trailer office which ran all over the district, had made him well known.
This was aided by Corinne's efforts and attendance at every sort of function in the District, including dinners, teas, weddings, anniversary parties

and funerals. Despite seeming to be ever-present in the District, Silvio attained a 100% voting attendance record in his first term. His legislative record, along with his service to his people, made him the best known political figure in Western Massachusetts. He won the Republican nomination for the Congressional seat without opposition. His campaign slogan was: Forceful—Progressive—Outspoken.

He was challenged by William H. Burns, a Holyoke alderman who had challenged Congressman Heselton in 1952. The first task of the Conte campaign was to clarify the fact that his opponent was not Professor Burns. There was no contest. Burns even offered to withdraw two and one-half weeks prior to the election if Silvio would join the Democratic Party and pledge support to Presidential candidate Kennedy. Silvio just kept campaigning and won 68.7% of the vote carrying each of the 84 towns in the district including Holyoke, a Democratic stronghold and Burns' hometown.

In the 1962 election, Silvio attained a vote percentage of 74.4%, the highest percentage attained by any of the 175 contested Republicans throughout the country. In 1964, Silvio's Democratic opponent had his ballot petition invalidated and had to run in the primary on a sticker campaign, a write-in campaign where supporters distribute stickers, printed with the candidate's name, to be affixed to the ballot on election day. Silvio also decided to run in the Democratic primary and took 83% of the vote. In the November election, with both party nominations, Silvio decided to be known as a Republican/Democrat. This election was the first of five consecutive elections in which Silvio had no opponent.

In 1968 a Republican minister decided to run in the Democratic primary to be able to challenge Silvio in November. Silvio, too, decided to enter this primary, again on a sticker campaign, and received 93% of the vote. Because appropriate documents were not filed on time, Silvio ran only as a Republican in November. After five uncontested runs, Silvio finally had a challenger in 1974, in part because of the Watergate aftermath and in part because of Silvio's opposition to the Dickey-Lincoln project. Silvio attained 71.6% of the vote, a landslide to most, but uncomfortably close for Silvio.

In 1976 Silvio had two opponents, both Northampton Democrats. There was still some animosity left from Watergate. Many people did not agree with Silvio's belief that the process should be allowed to work and wanted Nixon out much more quickly. Coupled with this was a strong anti-incumbent sentiment. The 1976 campaign began with Silvio in Washington and the two Democrats, O'Brien and McColgan attacking each other. O'Brien, who attacked Silvio as a "smokescreen liberal," won the primary by 50 votes out of 40,000+ cast. The challenger, McColgan, demanded a recount and several days later, was declared the winner by 11 votes. McColgan promptly challenged Silvio to four debates. Silvio refused saying, "I was tied up until last Saturday where I think I played an important part in last minute legislation. I have only 26 days in which to campaign while my opponent has been swinging away at me since last April. I intend to use much of my time answering some of the charges made against me but I will do so according to a schedule that I and my organization laid out, not by a schedule that my opponent would arrange." As Silvio's son John, a strong participant in the '76 campaign, recalls Silvio saying, "Why should I give my opponent all that exposure?" Instead, Conte sent one of his staff members, Jeff Jacobs, to debate McColgan at various gatherings, a tactic that infuriated McColgan.

Running against Silvio was an impossible task. Many of the attacks against him generated ill will toward his opponent. After each barrage many letters supporting Silvio appeared in the papers. When McColgan was supported by a local sport club, Silvio's friend and hunting pal, sports columnist Frank Sousa, wrote, "I felt ill, the sickest I'd felt since eating a prune pierogi." After describing Silvio's many environmental achievements, Frank echoed his sentiments of many western Massachusetts residents who adored their congressman, "I do not plan to use his record for backing him. I believe in the man because of the way his eyes light up in the field and the way he combs a small dog's ears with his fingers."

A few days before the election Silvio agreed to debate in Pittsfield at the General Electric plant, very friendly turf for Silvio who knew most of the people who worked there. McColgan made a number of charges against Silvio about financial disclosure and opposition to certain legislation. Silvio replied that he had given more complete financial disclosure than his opponent and went on to describe in detail why he had voted against some legislation and why he had backed other bills more beneficial to Massachusetts. His best campaigner, Corinne, whom everyone in the district loved, visited every town in Franklin county. Silvio, his family and friends were ever-present throughout the district. Silvio, fearing defeat, received just over 63% of the vote, carrying every town and city except Amherst.

The 1976 election sent challengers a strong message because in 1978

Silvio had no opponent. The 1980 election brought Silvio a Democratic opponent, a party committeewoman named Helen "Poppy" Doyle from Ashfield. Silvio once again was running on his record. He stated that the major issues were inflation, unemployment and foreign policy. Mrs. Doyle stated that the major issues were inflation and creation of jobs, particularly through improvement of rail lines. This was odd because Silvio was the nation's leading advocate and proponent of rail rehabilitation, especially in the Northeast.

Mrs. Doyle also charged that Silvio was out of touch with the district because he had discontinued operation of his mobile office van, a step which he said was taken because it made no sense to operate a vehicle which got eight miles to the gallon in a time of fuel scarcity. In a debate "Poppy" Doyle charged that Silvio was ineffective and out of touch. To this charge, Silvio responded, "Poppycock, ill-founded and ridiculous. You have to be either blind or deaf to believe a statement like that. All you have to do is go out in the street and ask the people." Doyle attacked Silvio's charge of "Poppycock" as sexist and rude to which he replied, "Poppycock is a word commonly used to mean garbage." As in the past this opponent learned that it was not beneficial to attack because Silvio would turn assaults into good press. All people remembered from this debate was Silvio saying "Poppycock." The 1980 election gave Silvio 74.8% of the vote.

In 1982 Silvio had a Democratic challenger, Mary Wentworth from Amherst. Silvio decided to run in the Democratic primary, won, and had no opponent once again. Some Republicans tried to persuade Silvio to run for the Senate seat being vacated by Paul Tsongas in 1984 because they feared losing control of the Senate but Silvio opted to stay in the House and was challenged by Mary Wentworth, who had received the Eleanor Roosevelt award. Mrs. Roosevelt's son, James, who had served in Congress with Silvio said that Silvio deserved the award. "I daresay that if anyone should be honored for devoting a career to the causes of peace and humanitarianism for which my mother toiled for so many years, it would be Silvio Conte." When Mrs. Wentworth announced that she offered "a chance to cast a vote for peace and justice" Silvio got a rebuttal from his friend, Joseph Addabbo, the Democratic Defense Appropriations Subcommittee Chairman who wrote a letter saying that Silvio was one of the leading members against "dangerously destabilizing weapons and wasteful defense spending."

Despite newspaper stories saying that he would be easily re-elected,

Silvio took nothing for granted. With Congress in session until mid-October, there was limited time to campaign, but Silvio went all over the district. "You just have to impress upon people that more guys have been beat after 20 or 30 years. A lot of guys who didn't worry, didn't come back." He won with 72.9% of the vote. Shortly into his new term there were discussions of his taking the one job he might have considered, Commissioner of Baseball, but this did not happen.

In 1986 Silvio had a new opponent, a Democratic consultant and former Congressional staffer named Robert Weiner, who charged that Silvio was nothing but a Reagan representative. Again Silvio followed his own course and refused to debate. His opponent alleged that Silvio had taken bribes for fixing revoked driver's licenses and for dining with reputed organized crime leaders, five years earlier. He showed written statements from two restaurant busboys whose signatures along with that of the notary were obliterated. This attack provoked Silvio's intense anger. "The groundless personal attack on me, my reputation, my record, my Italian heritage is without any basis or foundation." These charges went nowhere and Silvio continued to frustrate his opponent by ignoring him and going about the district seeing his people in his usual manner. For these efforts he received 78.1% of the vote.

In 1988 a new challenger came forth from Easthampton, saying that Silvio was no longer in touch. Silvio finally replied, "Every opponent who's run against me says that when they have no issues. I've never missed a parade in my many years. I've spent every weekend running up and down my district. They even made me an honorary policeman in Greenfield."

Silvio established an extraordinary political base. Seldom is a Congressional district with a large registered majority of one party dominated by a candidate of the minority. Silvio did this for many years. The 1988 figures are illustrative. In the Presidential race the Democratic candidate, Massachusetts Governor Michael Dukakis, received 58.1% of the vote in Silvio's district. Silvio, the Republican candidate for Congress, received 82.2% of the vote in a district with only 22.3% Republican registration. This electoral success gave Silvio great political strength. It allowed him to be independent and vote his conscience, knowing that his people would support him if he clearly explained his often difficult stands. He could challenge his own party and vote often with the Democrats as he did 75% of the time in 1987. It allowed him to speak out on the direction the Republicans were taking.

At the 1988 convention he said of the conservatives, "They want to see a party of purists kowtowing to their ideology, and they don't care if they bring the party down to defeat. I have to deal with it every day in Congress, and I always tell those birds, if you were in my district, you wouldn't be able to get elected dog catcher."

With campaigns of volunteers passing out leaflets and trinkets, setting up lawn signs and going door to door, the need for funds was low. Advertising was limited to occasional radio and newspaper spots. He did not use consultants or pollsters. He went directly to the people, his people. This allowed freedom from special interests. His success gave him time to do his work. In Washington he concentrated on legislation and did not run all over town to fund raisers. At home it gave him time to meet and listen to his people. At all-day office hour marathons he listened to what everyone had to say. This not only reinforced his popularity, it also kept him abreast of the people's views and concerns. He was an intense listener who heard what people said and took these concerns to Washington. He forged a deep and affectionate bond with his people through frequent and consistent contact.

Congressman Conte with former President Ford and former Speaker O'Neill at Silvio's 1987 testimonial dinner in Washington. *Vincent D'Addario Photograph*

Silvio and 2nd District Congressman Edward Boland at "roast" conducted by Mark Russell in Springfield, MA, 1988.
Vincent D'Addario Photograph

Congressman Conte with Nelson Mandela, late 1980s. *Conte Family Photograph*

Silvio at the 1989 dedication of the Conte Forum at Boston College. Tip O'Neill is telling him, "I'd rather have a library than a gym." *Vincent D'Addario Photograph*

Silvio with close friend, House Republican Leader, Robert Michel, 1989. *Conte Family Photograph*

Congressman Conte with President and Mrs. Bush. *Conte Family Photograph*

Corinne and Silvio on their 41st wedding anniversary, 1988.
Vincent D'Addario Photograph

Congressman Conte with Secretary of State James Baker at the 1990 Conte Issues Symposium. *Conte Family Photograph*

Silvio with Sandy Thomas of Greenfield, MA after a meeting regarding Attention Deficit Disorder, 1990. *Conte Family Photograph*

Conte family together at Gayle's wedding, 1989. *Conte Family Photograph*

The Berkshire Eagle

CITY & TOWN

Thursday, July 3, 1986

FUTURE CONGRESSMAN'S MOTHER, Lucy Lora, front row, and her sister, Mary, at boarding house at 45 Furnace St., North Adams. It was run by Angela Lora, Rep. Silvio O. Conte's grandmother. The men, Italian immigrants, were working on the Hoosac Tunnel. Conte's father, Ottavio, who died in 1971, was one of the tunnel crew. Conte's mother died in 1967.

Journey to opportunity

A congressman recounts parents' immigration

Reprint of 1986 Berkshire Eagle article which Silvio wrote about his parents coming to America. This article was written to commemorate the 100th Anniversary of the Statue of Liberty.

By Silvio O. Conte

I remember sitting at the kitchen table of our house in the ___ewood section of Pittsfield.

I was just a boy of 10 or 11, and my father, a big-hearted bear of a man, had just returned from a hard day of work at the General Electric Company's old porcelain plant. He was smiling from ear to ear.

"Why are you so happy tonight, Pa?" I asked him.

He shook his head from side to side and, in a thick Italian accent, said, "Tomorrow, Silvio, is the Fourth of July — birthday of freedom."

My father came to this country alone in 1905 at the age of 18 to find opportunity in the "land of the free."

Echoes of Ellis Island

When I was older, my father told me of the excitement, fear, joy and sorrow he remembered of his first hours on Ellis Island and of the wonder he felt in seeing the towering Statue of Liberty, after weeks at sea aboard a crowded cargo ship.

In the cavernous, echo-filled processing chambers at Ellis Island, the questions came fast and furiously, he recalled, from blue-jacketed strangers who spoke in a tongue he knew nothing of. Their crude and impersonal manner left mothers crying and fathers scrambling to keep their families together.

Those with enough money, their health and a little savvy made it through the madness to the ferry to Manhattan.

My mother's earliest memories of America began one cold, rainy day as a young girl of 8 or 9. She was taken with her two brothers from their home in Vecenza, Italy, to the docks of a French shipping port, where thousands of people waited in long lines to board battered, ill-equipped trade ships converted for human cargo.

They were going to join her father, who had left some time earlier for America, to establish a home and make enough money to send for his family.

Officials decided my uncle, then only a very small child, was too ill to make the passage to America. The trip had been years in the planning. My grandmother sent my mother and uncle back to Vecenza with a family friend, and the rest boarded the ship.

When my uncle recovered, the two small children were sent for. They were entrusted to the care of an older man. Unfortunately, he was unable to fulfill his duties because he was deathly ill with sea sickness throughout the voyage.

Woke to the statue

The ship's male and female passengers were separated for the crossing, and the two children, just 8 and 10 years old, were moved to different parts of the ship.

They were allowed to visit during the day, when they played together on deck, but had to fend for themselves at night.

. After weeks of storms and the loneliness of long nights alone in the communal chambers of the battered old ship, the children rose one morning to frantic calls in many languages: New York could be seen from the upper deck.

My mother said everyone rushed to the deck to catch a glimpse of the huge statue they had been told of, and recounted the eerie silence as hundreds of faces stared into the distance, caught in the awe of America.

The children were shuffled roughly through the Ellis Island processing line. Alone and frightened, they gave their names to a young man in a blue jacket, who told them to stay where they were until he returned. A short time later, he arrived with another similarly clad official and a tall imposing figure wearing a bushy moustache and carrying a bag of fruit.

"Do you recognize this man," one of the men asked, pointing to the stranger.

"No" they replied, "We've never seen him before."

The stranger was dismayed and deeply hurt that his own children did not recognize him. But that was typical of what immigrants endured in order to bring their families to America.

Frightened that his children would be returned to Italy because of mistaken identity, he returned to his home in North Adams to find a lawyer to plead his case. After more than a week of internment in the cold, lonely Ellis Island processing chambers, the children finally rejoined their family and set out for the Berkshires and their new lives in America.

In the tunnel, in the mill

America grew up, in many ways, during the early 1900s, and much of this country's tremendous growth came through the efforts of young, dynamic immigrants, looking to realize their dreams in the land of the free.

My father found work on a dangerous but boldly enterprising venture called the Hoosac Tunnel in North Adams. North Adams was also my mother's home, and after a year in school she went to work spinning thread in the old Greylock Mills.

After walking the four miles to work every day, she operated seven thread spinning machines, walked four miles home and spent the evening helping her mother run a boarding house that became home to men working on the Hoosac Tunnel.

It was at the boarding house that my mother met the hard-working, kind-hearted Italian wayfarer who would become her husband and my father. Always looking for opportunity and willing to work any hours, Pa later found employment at GE's porcelain plant and worked his way up to foreman, supervising a crew of more than 70 men.

He used to take me down to the plant with him from time to time, and he always beamed with pride in the company and his accomplishments. Like so many fiercely optimistic new Americans, my father knew that this country offered no free lunches, no easy deals.

But it offered one very precious commodity, and offers it to this day — opportunity.

Rep. Conte is attending the 100th birthday celebration of the Statue of Liberty tomorrow and is visiting Ellis Island "to go and see for myself what my parents saw from crowded passenger ships 80 years ago."

ADVOCATE FOR THE CONGRESS

"The primary role of a Congressman is
as a trustee for the nation."
—*Silvio O. Conte, 1969*

Silvio Conte had the reverence for Congress that Harry Truman
had for the Presidency. His deep devotion to the Congress arose from the
intense pride he first felt in January of 1959 when he, the son of Italian immigrants, walked up the Capitol steps to take the oath of office. He retained
this pride, this respect throughout his career.

In 1965, when Voting Rights legislation, which Silvio strongly supported, was pending, President Johnson announced, "I will send to Congress a law." Silvio was infuriated that the President viewed the Congress
as a rubber stamp and said, "A law, mind you, not a proposal, not a plan,
not a suggestion, not a bill, but a law, a foregone conclusion, a decree." Silvio
opposed President Nixon on impoundments, Executive Branch refusals to
spend appropriated funds, and said, "The crucial issue facing the Congress
is the gradual erosion of power to the Executive Branch. The approval of
legislation granting the President authority to cut spending to a $250 billion
level was an unfortunate and dangerous abdication of the Congressional
Constitutional power of the purse."

Attacks upon the institution, attacks which became increasingly stri-
dent in the 1980s, were a source of personal distress for Silvio, especially
when they came from Members. His answer always was, "Let's do the job
we're elected to do." Silvio strongly disagreed when fellow members tried
to legislate away Congressional authority and staunchly fought attempts to
cede Congressional responsibility. James Madison wrote in Federalist Paper No. 39 almost 200 years earlier, "Among a people consolidated into one
nation, the supremacy is completely vested in the National Legislature."

Silvio clearly understood that Article I of the Constitution delegates spending and other powers to the Congress and was as eloquent as the Federalist papers when he said of the executive branch in 1982, "I don't think they understand the process. They'd like to think they can come up here and tell us what the committee should do or should not do. We're elected by the people, half a million people, not to become robots but to think for ourselves, to be independent human beings to do what is right for them and for the country."

James Madison would have nodded in agreement as Silvio explained how the process should function. "You have to give a little and take a little, just like seasoning food. When I first came here everybody in the hall knew each other. It was like one big family whether they were Republican or Democrat. Now you never see these people any more. They're all campaigning and they're all thinking up ideas of how they're going to take over the world or the Congress. It's important to have some around here who know the House, the Rules of the House, what you can do with give and take and know the art of compromise."

With this he spelled out his personal style of doing this. "I do get excited and I am emotional, but when it's over, I slap him on the back and invite him over for a drink. I give it everything I've got but I laugh afterward. I enjoy it. I like a good give and take."

Silvio's dismay was aroused by talk of the line item veto and the balanced budget amendment. He often said that the line item veto makes the President a king. As for the balanced budget amendment, he asked why take years to do what should be started now. His ire peaked with the introduction and passage of Gramm-Rudman or "Grim Rudman" as he called it. The idea that Congress would give up its most important and basic spending function to some automatically targeted formula was unthinkable and unconscionable. "Power would be delegated to bean counters. I don't know about you, but I'm not ready to surrender my vote to a bureaucrat's red pen. My complaint is we're elected by the people, the taxpayers in our districts to come here a do a job. I don't think anyone elected me to come here to Washington to push a button to make things work. They want me to make tough decisions. That's what Gramm-Rudman does, it pushes a button. If you don't reach a certain target by October 1, Gramm-Rudman goes into effect and cuts across the board. What happens is that you are cutting good programs as well as bad programs. We should have the will, the determination, the guts to make these cuts ourselves."

Some said that Silvio opposed Gramm-Rudman because it threatened his clout and the programs for which he had a hand in appropriating funds. While he was alarmed by the possibility and the inevitability of this happening, he was more alarmed by the destruction of the constitutional role of the Congress, so alarmed that he joined 10 other colleagues and challenged this legislation before the Supreme Court. He was pleased that two months after the passage of Gramm-Rudman, the Supreme Court struck down the sequestration provisions. "Fortunately, part of that monster, the sequestration provision, was slain by the court today."

Silvio continued to battle Gramm-Rudman along with the Budget Reconciliation Act of 1974 because they both served to prolong the legislative process and to prevent the Congress from acting in a timely fashion. "We will not only resolve, reconcile, authorize, and appropriate, we will now reconsider. If four or five votes on the same issue aren't enough to bring this institution to its knees, we will now vote six times."

Gramm-Rudman further complicated an already difficult process. Unlimited Senate amendments enraged Silvio and frequently provoked Presidential veto. "Any bill that goes over to the Senate has to be amended to death. Everybody has to have a little claim of authorship. If Moses were alive today and he was walking up the Mount with his little tablet and chisel and hammer and banging out the Ten Commandments he'd never reach the top because those Senators over there would be tugging at his robe saying, "Hey, wait a minute, I've got an amendment."

The lack of timeliness created another disaster—the Continuing Resolution—the legislation making temporary appropriations because the regular annual legislation appropriating all government funds was not approved by the start of the fiscal year. Continuing Resolutions were needed every year for several years in a row. In the midst of the 1984 Presidential campaign he said:

> "For two days now the political gurus have debated the Louisville debate over and over again. This Congress is determined to debate anything but the Continuing Resolution. Now Mr. Speaker, I want to ask you the question. Are we better off than we were two weeks ago? After two hours and hours of conferences and four extensions. The Conferees are still in Senate 207 sitting on their, well I can't say

it, but in rhymes with the almost extinct fish, the bass. One of the most important jobs this Congress is elected to perform is passing the Federal Budget. We are now 10 days into the Fiscal Year. We haven't approved the Continuing Resolution let alone a regular Appropriations package. We become the laughingstock, day in and day out. It's the same old question. Not where's the beef, but where's the pork. Let's get the pig in the pen and the show on the road."

Year after year he introduced legislation to repeal Gramm-Rudman and the Budget Act of 1974 saying in one debate, "we're in a morass, we're in a barrel of molasses, we can't legislate." Not only did Continuing Resolutions become annual affairs but also they took more and more time to get resolved. In 1987 it appeared that the Congress might have to stay in session through Christmas, a frightening thought to Silvio who so looked forward to being with all of his family at home in Pittsfield. At 1:00 a.m. during the debate he gave an eloquent assessment of the situation and its effects, concluding with one of his poems to urge the Congress to act and act now.

"Mr. Speaker, we're considering a Conference Agreement that provides $450 billion for the Appropriations bills for the remainder of the fiscal year. We should be discussing the fiscal and policy issues in that agreement. But we won't talk about the issues. We'll talk about a legislative process that denies the members of this House the opportunity to vote on these issues. We're going to have one vote on these issues. We're going to have one vote on the Conference Agreement of over 2,000 pages which not a single member has read or understands. Who's responsible for this? In Pogo's immortal words, "We have met the enemy and it is us." We created the Budget Act. We created Gramm-Rudman-Hollings. We created televised proceedings, Political Action Committees, party caucus rules and other reforms which expose members to pressure from special interests. We created a process where it would be difficult under the best of circumstances for a majority to lead effectively. The members of this House are intelligent, honorable men and women who have come here to make public policy and who will make responsible decisions in an open process if given that opportunity. If we continue to deny them that opportunity they will leave public life as many have done already and we will have denied this House and our Country an entire generation of new, bright leaders. We don't enact Appropriations Bills because we have the Budget Act and Gramm-Rudman-Hollings which we use so effectively to give the appearance of a timely and responsible legislative process. I've drafted a bill to repeal those two laws. Dozens of members have come to me on the floor and said, "You're right." I have one co-sponsor, my good friend from Indiana, John Myers, and I have picked up another tonight. That tells you all you need to know about the problem and solution. Mr. Speaker, that concludes my partici-pation in the ritual flogging of this process. I take this problem and my job very seriously, but I can't say the same for the most of the proposed solutions.

I scratched out as I sat here something on the lighter side and it goes something like this:

'Twas four nights before Christmas and all through the House
Every member sat waiting until the coming of the cows.
The President pondered, black pen in hand.
What Congress is doing I don't understand.
When the fiscal year started over two months ago.
The people expected a Christmastime show.
The Senate has dawdled at the pace of a snail.
The House has responded with a long anguished wail.
Is there any one person who can rescue our cause?
The answer was clear, it would be old Santa Claus.
Then out of the dome there arose such a clatter.
I sprang from the well to see what was the matter.
Away through the chamber I flew on my cart.
Down the hall, up the ramp then I stopped with a start.
There up in the scaffolding high in the air.
Was a livid St. Nick who cried with despair.
O Whitten, O Natcher, O Michel, O Wright.
O Conte, O Foley let's finish tonight.
His warning was heeded on a spirited note.

All members lined up to cast their final vote.
And then the two bills tied up in the sleigh.
The members all cheered and he went on his way.
And I heard him exclaim and he flew out of sight.
Merry Christmas to all and to all a good night."

While no one in the Congress worked harder or longer than Silvio, he dreaded becoming bogged down in the same matters over and over. The process had overtaken the issues. He offered practical clear-cut solutions. "I have a simple way. It's so simple I can't get anybody to support me. At the beginning of the year we get a projection of the revenue. That is the target to live within for the 13 Appropriations bills. We change the Rules of the House so that all 13 bills would be brought to the desk and voted on together. That would give us the necessary discipline to live within."

It was his view that the deficit could only be cured by hard work, hard choices, difficult cuts and higher revenues.

BOSS

"He was a real piece of work".
—*Nan Donnelly, Office Manager, Pittsfield*

Silvio Conte had the reputation for being the toughest, most impossible boss on Capitol Hill. To his staff he could be demanding, difficult, petulant and unreasonable. They said he was "like LBJ and wanted their whole soul." His looks could kill. He was formidable. He loved to catch them goofing off. Long-time office manager Fran McGuire said, "fortunately he made so much noise coming down the hall that we knew when he was near."

He was unrelenting with staff time off. One day Fran finally accepted a two year old luncheon invitation to go out while Silvio was fishing in Alaska. Just before dessert she was paged in a restaurant and he was on the line laughing, "When the cat's away, the mice will play." He would holler "Hey-yo-yo" to the outer office and two or three people would appear at his desk. He could call at 6 a.m. on the Fourth of July to have someone go into the office to get him a telephone number. He would read a prepared speech or position paper and say, "It sounds like a term paper I wrote in 1947." One detailed speech on Social Security prepared with extensive research was tossed into a snow bank along a Western Massachusetts road enroute to being delivered because it was "too technical and complicated. I'll just think of something else."

Yet Silvio had the most dedicated, hard working and loyal people on Capitol Hill. He had many people who served him for years. He sought out good individuals, gave them challenging assignments, listened to their findings and opinions. While he sought hard working people, none worked harder or longer than he did. He toiled right alongside. His demands built a cohesiveness in the staff. They needed to work together to help each other survive. They sometimes took the blame for each other.

The worst thing that could befall a staffer was to be on the road in the district with Silvio and be approached by a constituent saying that they were disappointed not to receive a reply to a recent request. Silvio would become livid and start screaming at whomever he had brought from the office whether that person was at fault or not. The usually efficient system of taking every request on 3x5 note cards had failed. Sometimes the onus would be lifted right way if Silvio winked. Otherwise, once back in the car Silvio would say, "Hey make sure you take care of that, will ya?" Although the first request may have gone astray, the second was followed up with speed and intensity.

Staff filled many functions for Silvio. They gathered intelligence around the House, telling him what other members were working on and what they wanted. He needed them to work longer hours than other staffers because he worked longer hours. He spent a great deal of time on the House floor and in committee hearings and would wait until the end of day to begin constituent work which for him was very involved. Beyond routine items, Social Security, veteran and immigration matters, Silvio helped people get jobs, housing, schooling and even gave advice to people. He did not abide half-hearted efforts. He and his staff followed through, sometimes for years, until the proper conclusion was achieved.

He used staff as props sometimes. On the House floor members would approach him with amendments for their pet projects. When Silvio saw this, sometimes he would start screaming at his staff saying that they were all incompetent and that if they knew anything he would be President by now. Hearing this, other members would turn away, holding their projects for another day. Silvio would wink at his people to indicate success.

A staffer could be a foil in a large battle. One year at a House-Senate Conference to work out final agreements on the annual spending package for the entire Federal government, all was resolved except for the battle over silver price supports. Westerners were holding out for a high support price and wanted the government to purchase more silver for the stockpile to keep miners working. Easterners like Silvio who had industries which used silver wanted a lower price. By 3 a.m. all the conferees were screaming for settlement so Silvio said, "I've got a silver expert," and called his office and said, "Colonel, get down here and bring all the silver papers." When he arrived Silvio said, "Let's settle this." He took the Senator along with his aide, Chinch Wollerton, into a closet.

Silvio started arguing, saying that he could not live with these high prices. "What do you propose?" After the first suggestion Silvio planted his foot down on the top of Chinch's foot and said, "Well, Colonel, will that work?" Knowing nothing about silver but aware of an acute pain in his instep, he replied no. After several compromises by the Senator and painful "no" responses, the Senator shouted, "I can't go any lower than this." "Well, what do you think?" Silvio asked as he removed his foot. Taking the elimination of pain as a positive sign, the reply was, "That should work." Silvio then said "Get with the staff and work out the details. That takes care of that."

Sometimes an aide provided clothing. Frequently Silvio would rise very early and go hunting or fishing before the Congress began its daily session. One day he came into his office wearing fishing waders. He went through his closet looking for a clean shirt and tie and dress shoes. Finding none, he hollered "Hey, Jim get in here. Gimme your shirt, tie and shoes. I gotta be on the Floor in five minutes." Jim Phelan had to work in a T-shirt and barefoot all day.

For a staffer, working for Silvio was an unique adventure. Because he was involved in so many legislative details, they, too, were deeply involved. He was always moving forward and made the staff part of the effort. He did not maintain a chain of command. People could go directly to him with questions or suggestions. He was as open and accessible to his staff as he was to his constituents. He took many fresh from college or law school, some even coming as summer interns before graduation, and molded them into hard working, effective legislative professionals.

Many Conte staffers have related how they received great respect and many opportunities because they worked for Silvio Conte. Although Silvio was frugal in dispensing praise to his staff, he had great pride in their accomplishments, often pointing out to friends that his people were all over Washington, both in and out of government. His people achieved many notable positions. The most extraordinary was not an American, but a British woman who came to work for Silvio in 1960. Betty Boothroyd came to America and worked for the Democrats in the Kennedy Presidential campaign and wanted to work in the Congress. This was difficult, not being American, and the Democrats for whom she had worked found her no position, so Silvio hired her to earn passage home. After initially giving her trivial office work to do, he decided to see how much she could accomplish. He gave her what he thought would be several days work which she finished by four o'clock the same day. After that he told people that she could do more work that anyone else. Upon her return to Britain she eventually ran for the House of Commons and became its first woman Speaker.

Despite his tough demeanor, Silvio cared about his employees, even the ones who did not perform as he wished. On hunting trips he sometimes would complain about a staffer doing this or not doing that. After he complained bitterly about one staff member on two successive trips one of his pals asked, "Why not just fire him?" To this Silvio replied, "I haven't found him a job yet." The staffers became part of his extended family. He fed them at the family table, took them on trips, invited them to parties, went to their weddings, children's christening and so forth. When they left his employ they stayed in touch, always invited to his annual birthday party at the Botanic Garden. As long time aide Willa Rawls Dumas said, "We would laugh at him, talk about him, complain about him, but we loved him dearly. We had more fun than anyone on Capitol Hill."

FAREWELL

"So long, old pal."
—*"Tip" O'Neill, 1991*

*A*fter the 1988 election Silvio entered the hospital to have replacement surgery on one knee. Walking had become increasingly painful. Old football knee injuries coupled with arthritis made Silvio ride around the Capitol corridors on an electric cart with the American and Italian flags flying on the back, beeping the cart's horn to signal his approach. The surgery did not eliminate the cart because only one knee was replaced but some pain was relieved.

But Silvio lost none of his humor. At his annual birthday party in Washington with the theme, "Mallard Fillmore—The Duck Stops Here", he told friends from home, "This has been a rough year. I have undergone two surgeries. Guys are lining up in Northampton and Amherst ready to take my seat over. It's really great to be here. A guy asked me the other day if I bought any IBM stock. Hell at my age I don't even buy green bananas anymore. Just taking it one day at a time."

His intensity and passion remained undiminished as he added, "People say to me, don't you think it's time to slow down and perhaps pass the baton on to someone else? My response is it will not be my time to slow down until every child in this country has the opportunity to receive an education he or she is entitled to."

Silvio looked forward to the Bush Presidency with great enthusiasm. He strongly agreed with George Bush's pledges to be the "Environmental President" and the "Education President." And there was the personal side, as Silvio said in a C-SPAN interview, "George and I have been friends since he was in the Congress 25 years ago. He played for my baseball team. He played first base for me."

The Bush years proved to be difficult because new initiatives were thwarted by the deficit. Yet Silvio forged ahead. Beyond getting President Bush to support the study of acid rain and sign the Clean Air Act of 1990, Silvio introduced, got passed by the Congress and convinced the President to sign the North American Wetlands Act of 1989. This act authorized the Federal government to purchase two million acres of wetlands. In 1989 Silvio got an appropriation of $25 million to begin this effort.

In February, 1989 Silvio was both thrilled and proud when Boston College dedicated its new athletic complex as The Silvio O. Conte Forum to express appreciation for the many years of help. For Silvio this was an extremely emotional event. It was clear evidence that he fulfilled his 1947 promise to succeed. He was proud to have this impressive and well known structure prominently displaying his name with the Thomas P. O'Neill Library nearby.

Beyond this pride was Silvio's belief that his success arose from his Boston College Jesuit education. He often said that BC taught him to work long and hard in a disciplined manner. His strong independence was grounded in this Jesuit education. The BC motto, "Ever to Excel," became his own as his children who frequently heard it can readily attest. Tip O'Neill also spoke at his dedication and said that "All things considered, I would rather have a library than a gym."

Budget issues continued to occupy much of Silvio's time during 1989 and 1990. Concern over mounting deficits threatened to curtail many programs. Silvio worked tirelessly to preserve funding for areas important to him, especially bio-medical research, the student loan program and low income heating assistance. He also was vigorous in taking initiatives to pare expenditures. He sponsored legislation to investigate savings and loan defaults. He was particularly irate because the entire nation was funding what he saw as a southwestern problem. He also fought the Supercollider and B-2 Bomber.

In 1990 he authored the Antarctica Protection and Conservation Act. After the Exxon Valdez disaster in Alaska, he became concerned about the future of the world's last remaining unspoiled continent. This legislation was unique because it was initiated by Silvio in January of 1990 and signed into law in November of the same year. The legislation, which provided for a prohibition of any drilling or mining in Antarctica and some funds for cleanup, was championed by Silvio with the battle cry, "Why can't we do this?" He testified at committee hearings on the bill, managed it on the House floor and persuaded President Bush to sign it.

Lack of agreement on the Budget prevented Appropriations bills from being passed on time, causing the several threats of government shutdown. These struggles caused many additional meetings for the senior members of Congress and kept Silvio in Washington much of the time. This gave him the opportunity to develop a close relationship with his young grandson, Nicholas, son of Silvio and Corinne's daughter Sylvia, who lived nearby. One day in the office Silvio overheard someone say, "There's no one named Nonno (Italian for grandfather) here." Silvio bellowed, "Hey, I'm the Nonno around here. Put those calls through to me right away!"

The Budget struggles led to the 1990 Budget Summit with top members of Congress in conference secluded at Andrews Air Force Base in extended meetings with the Administration, sometimes with President Bush. Agreement which resulted in the President breaking his "No new taxes" pledge finally came in the fall after months of rancor. Silvio often told Corinne that he was dismayed that more could not be done to curb spending, especially runaway entitlements.

One day in the midst of a heated and angry debate Silvio sat across from a row of pens with Presidential Seals lined up in front of President Bush and suddenly hollered, "Stop, stop. Hey George, gimme some of those pens. I'm having a picnic up at Mt. Tom this weekend and I can get 40 bucks apiece for them." After Silvio scooped up a few, the debate went forward with tension lessened. In early October the budget agreement finally went to the House floor more than a week after the start of the new fiscal year. Prompt action once again was needed to prevent a government shutdown. At 1:00 a.m. Silvio delivered his plea to move the process along.

> In fourteen hundred and ninety two
> Columbus sailed the ocean blue.
> Through storms and gales and fiercest seas
> And armed with foreign subsidies
> He came upon this brave new land,
> Just he and his intrepid band.
> In nineteen-ninety here we are.
> I don't think we have come so far.
> We scream and moan and boo and hiss.

We don't have time to take . . . a break.
We shout and jeer and fuss and bark.
We blame each other in the dark.
Although we have five centuries
We see no forest for the trees.
We're frightened by the interest groups.
We act like silly nincompoops.
We can't make cuts that cause some sting.
We cannot even do a thing.
And now we have run out of time
And that, dear friends, is our only crime.
The government - it has shut down
And we're the only game in town.
Let's work to get this budget through
And get these tourists to the zoo.
If Christopher were here tonight
He'd be astounded by our fight.
He'd know not why we can't agree.
It seems so elementary.
We're in such deep financial trouble,
That we will have to burst the bubble.
Home heating oil must be tax free
And we can't hurt the elderly.
Incentives that will make some sense
Could get this body off the fence.
And this is how I end my poem.
Let's pass something and then go ho-em".

Once the budget reconciliation and appropriations bills were passed, Silvio had nine days to campaign for the 1990 Election. His opponent frequently attacked him as being out of touch, a sentiment in part fueled by some of the local papers which gave little coverage of the Budget Summit. At Silvio's late summer picnic at Mt. Tom a reporter asked Silvio about what he thought about his opponent saying he was too old, out of touch and should retire. Silvio replied, "What's that guy's name anyway?" Once he got back to Pittsfield he did his usual whirlwind campaigning, going everywhere. He generally ignored his opponent's attacks although one day he did reply "This guy is another world. I do more work and cover more bases in one day than he'll do in a lifetime." He also answered those who suggested retirement "To be honest I don't know what I would do with myself. I'd drive my wife crazy and climb the walls if I didn't have my work." Nine day's campaigning with no media advertisement or coverage produced almost 78% of the vote for Silvio. He related his concern over losing five percentage points from 1988, saying, "What have I done wrong?" to his friend Tip O'Neill, who replied, "You're out of your mind—don't worry about it."

A few weeks after the 1990 election, Silvio's prostate cancer began to spread rapidly. He began chemotherapy treatments, which were debilitating, but went to the Capitol every day. He was sent to a hospital support group to meet and talk with other cancer patients about problems with the disease but soon said, "I can't do this. I've got to go to work."

Because of these treatments he could only leave Washington to go to Pittsfield for one day for Christmas. Through January the disease progressed. Silvio introduced the legislation for the Connecticut River Wildlife Refuge. At the end of January he hosted a luncheon for the new Mayor of Washington, Sharon Pratt Dixon, who had come to his November birthday party where he promised to introduce her to some colleagues. As the *Boston Globe* said after he died "At the time, few could understand why, with his health failing fast, the white Republican from Pittsfield was helping out Dixon, the black Democratic mayor from Washington. The answer was simple: Conte kept his word, even as his days were short."

By mid-January the decision on whether or not to attack Iraq was before the House and Senate. There was extensive debate as the President pushed to pursue the conflict, awaiting Congressional endorsement. Silvio agonized for three days, trying to decide whether to support his old friend, President Bush, or vote to give sanctions some more time. He was wary of endorsing war escalation, reflecting back on the Gulf of Tonkin and Lebanon debacles. He finally decided that the conflict should wait a little longer and was one of only three Republicans to vote against the President. Once the vote went the other way, he got up on the House floor and said he was 100% behind the President.

On the first day of February Silvio was taken by Corinne to National Institutes of Health because he was experiencing some paralysis. The CT-Scan discovered a blood clot in the brain which was successfully removed, but then another developed, putting him into a coma from which he did not recover, passing away on February 8, 1991.

Up to the end he retained his perspective and humor. Knowing that his days were limited, he told Corinne, "Don't feel bad for me. I've done everything I ever wanted." Upon arrival at NIH he had been met by his doctors as he was wheeled into the lobby. In front of the crowd Silvio bellowed, "What the hell have you guys done? Two months ago I was in perfect health and now look at me." Once in his hospital room he was given a "Foley" catheter and said, "At least this place knows which side its bread is buttered on. I get a building named for me. All the Speaker gets is a catheter."

Upon his death, tributes poured in from everywhere. The most eloquent ones came from home where people said two things: "He never forgot that he came from Pittsfield" and "He helped everyone." The evening before his funeral, calling hours were held at All Souls Church on Pittsfield's east side where Silvio grew up. More than 7,000 people stood in 15 degree cold for two to three hours to say good-bye to their friend and neighbor. These were people whom he had helped with jobs, visas, passports, West Point appointments, business problems, family problems, housing.

They came because he had helped them and they loved him. They told how he always did the reading on Palm Sunday, how he came to Sunday Mass when he was in Pittsfield and had coffee with them after the service or went to someone's home on a Sunday afternoon to sit at the kitchen table to drink homemade wine and play cards. The next day he would get on a plane to Washington to go to the White House and explain what must be done to get some legislation passed. He gracefully and easily bridged the vast gap between the Beltway and Western Massachusetts because he was the same person in both places.

Silvio's funeral was held at St. Joseph's Church in Pittsfield. A delegation of more than 100 came from Washington led by Vice President Quayle and Speaker Foley. The church was full, the parish house overflowing and people lined the streets, the schools and many businesses were closed. The Funeral Mass was held on Ash Wednesday. Father George and Silvio's two closest friends from the Congress, Tip O'Neill and Bob Michel, were the speakers, giving eloquent, moving and humorous tributes.

The most moving and eloquent words came from Silvio's people. Along the road to the cemetery the procession passed a small boy holding a campaign sign simply saying, "Another Family for Conte." A month later a memorial service in the Capitol Rotunda and Special Orders of the House produced more tributes which described the ways in which Silvio had enriched the lives of the various speakers, how he had helped them, how he had made them laugh and how enthusiastic and energetic he was. Again, the best came from home—Senator Kennedy read a letter from Sandy Thomas of Greenfield, saying, "He was kind, gentle and good. Mr. Conte helped me try to obtain educational help for my child when I approached him two years ago. He literally held my hand throughout the entire time and never let go once."

EPILOGUE

*A*fter thirty-two years in the Congress, Silvio Conte left behind an abundant legislative accomplishment. Among the matters which he crafted or for which he served as patron saint were: Student Loan Program, Bio-Medical Research at NIH, Low Income Energy Assistance Program, AIDS Funding, Acid Rain Cleanup, Coast Guard, Amtrak, Smithsonian Institution, U.S. Fish & Wildlife Service, Migratory Bird Commission, Connecticut River cleanup, hundreds of thousands of acres of wetlands set aside as wildlife refuges, University of Massachusetts Polymer Center, Railroad rehabilitation funding, Antarctic Protection Act, Attention Deficit Disorder, the Postal Workers and funding for many specific diseases. Silvio devoted his attention to substance rather than ideology. His concerns were clear and consistent: quality of life issues such as health, education, environment and infrastructure. Silvio's time in Congress was spent moving ahead and looking for ways to make life better for the people he directly represented as well as those throughout the country. His view of his job was basic. Its purpose was to help people, especially those who had no one else to look after them. It was from this that he drew his greatest satisfaction.

Silvio demonstrated that there is great nobility in public service if the public interest is honestly and diligently served. He passionately believed in the American system of government. He was in full accord with the framers of the Constitution that the Congress was the most important branch of government and he fought with his full strength any attempts to diminish this. Silvio was cut from the cloth that the Founding Fathers intended. They did not give much thought to political parties—and neither did Silvio—they intended that representatives look after the concerns of all their constituents, and that is what he did. The most interesting question about Silvio Conte is how did he, a minority member of Congress for his entire 32 years there, manage to accomplish so much and how did he manage to be in the middle of every major spending matter for at least the last 10 years of his career? Was it because he worked harder and longer than anyone? Was it because of his boundless energy and enthusiasm? Was it because of his independence and flexibility grounded in rock solid support at home? Was it his superb preparation? Was it his personality? Was it his ability to bring out the best in people by making them feel a part of something larger than themselves? Was it his piercing blue eyes which said: "Go with me on this, you'll need me again soon?" Was it because he knew what everyone else wanted and why they wanted it? Was it because he instinctively comprehended the entire process and its players? Was it because most everything he espoused made good sense?

Much of Silvio's personality came from his Italian heritage. It made him emotional, passionate and sensitive. This Italian background gave him a broad and expansive perspective of the country and the world. His views were always broad. He came by this naturally, as described by Luigi Barzini in *The Italians*. "Italians have discovered America for the Americans, taught poetry, statesmanship and the rules of trade to the English; military art to the Germans; cuisine to the French; acting and ballet dancing to the Russians and music to everybody." Silvio was a true son of this tradition because he was vitally interested in everything. Yet, he was truly American, too. He patriotically and almost naively believed in the American system and ideals. To him everyone was equal. He was not caught up in the trappings of the Beltway. How many Congressional leaders are seen by their staff through the office window helping a delivery man across the street unload a bread truck?

Silvio was sometimes accused of voting with his heart or by the "seat of his pants." At a speech at Boston College he said "Those decisions, and there have been many over the past 28 years don't always come from experience or position papers or from staff expertise or even from common sense. Most decisions come straight from the heart." Yet his votes were carefully and sometimes agonizingly reasoned. His votes were also practical and realistic. He never was a politician who felt that if he could not have what he wanted then he would be against everything else. His attitude toward legislation always was if it is good, vote yes and if bad, vote no. If there was more good than bad, vote yes.

Silvio Conte gave the American people a great gift, even beyond his solid legislative accomplishments. In a troubled and often jaded time, he gave an extraordinary and sterling example of service as a representative of the people. He exerted on the public's behalf fantastic energy to try to do the job right. He served the people of Western Massachusetts and the nation for 32 years with hard work, devotion, energy, integrity, enthusiasm, passion and humor. He managed to do this while having more fun than anyone, extending his enjoyment and passion for life to those around him. He was well worthy of Tip O'Neill's comment to Corinne a few months after Silvio's death: "If the Founding Fathers came back and picked from our 200 year history one member of Congress to show how they intended the Congress to work, they would have selected Silvio Conte."

INDEX